AF489684

State Knows Best

A Memoir

Nicole Hayes

This is a work of nonfiction. Names and identifying details have been changed in some cases to protect the privacy of individuals. Certain scenes have been reconstructed from memory.

Second edition published 2026
Originally published 2025

Published by Nicole Hayes Books
Phoenix, Arizona

ISBN 979-8-9947040-0-4 (paperback)
ISBN 979-8-9947040-1-1 (epub)

Printed in the United States of America

Publisher's Cataloging-in-Publication Data

Names: Hayes, Nicole, 1987-, author.
Title: State knows best / Nicole Hayes.
Description: Phoenix, AZ: Nicole Hayes Books, 2026.
Identifiers: LCCN: 2026902477 | ISBN: 979-8-9947040-0-4 (paperback) | 979-8-9947040-1-1 (epub)
Subjects: LCSH Hayes, Nicole, 1987-. | Foster children–United States–Biography. | Adoption–United States–Biography. | Teenage pregnancy–United States. | Teenage mothers–United States–Biography. | BISAC BIOGRAPHY & AUTOBIOGRAPHY / Memoirs | FAMILY & RELATIONSHIPS / Adoption & Fostering

TABLE OF CONTENTS

Your Only Warning

This is a true story.

Not a fairy tale.

There are no glass slippers, no fairy godmothers, and no magical endings wrapped in satin bows.

No.

This is a rage-on-the-page memoir about how the state said it knew best—and it didn't.

How a teenager got chewed up by a system that claimed to protect her.

How "choice" was dangled in front of her like a carrot on a stick, while every exit sign was quietly blocked.

This is a warning.

A scream in print.

A survivor's note to the next girl in line.

You'll hear sarcasm.

You'll hear bitterness.

You'll hear grief and anger.

Because the system isn't broken—it's working exactly the way it was built.

Because people don't always want to help you—they want to manage you.

And because sometimes, the ones with power get to walk away feeling like saviors…

While the rest of us are left picking up pieces we never shattered.

So turn the page, if you dare.
But don't say I didn't warn you.

With Love, Rage, and Truth

Back Story, Or Whatever

There are plenty of valid reasons for me to lie on my bed in my cramped room — the one assigned to me by my newest foster parent — staring at the ceiling, angrily wishing everything about my life were different. I'm fifteen, and my life is in shambles. I suppose it's been that way since birth. The State took me away from my mother when I was still too young to remember her.

The State then placed me into scary foster homes with pervy dads and older brothers. Thankfully, I've gotten pretty good at blocking out a lot, but there's one foster home I can still vaguely remember.

There was a boy there. As I think about it now and try to recall, I don't think I ever knew his age. Maybe he was an adult — though to a young child, which I was at the time, any tall person is an adult. And to this day, I'm not 100% sure who he was, but I believe he was their older son. His name was Bobby, and all my mind will let me recall is that he would have me sit in his lap and turn on cartoons. Care Bears. Literally to this day, I don't want to see a damn koala bear or even a stuffed bear. And I have a slight memory of him coming into the room me and my sister slept in at night. But like I said, I managed to block out a lot.

These were State-licensed and "approved" homes! Homes where me and my sister would sometimes stay together, but mostly, we were separated while we waited for our mother to clean herself up.

Spoiler alert: she never did. And well, now she's dead. A lifetime of drug use eventually did her in. And in case you're wondering, "Well, what about your father?" — he was 23 when she was just 15, and he also had a drug addiction and was in and out of prison. I never got to meet him, even though I actually attempted to — twice.

Why did I even want to meet him? I'm not sure I even know. But he died of a fentanyl overdose.

So of course, with these two for parents, the State got involved.

They didn't get involved to help my mother, in my opinion. Which I think is what she actually needed — being just a child herself. Help. Support. Assistance. Maybe placed in a home herself, since clearly hers was not suitable.

But of course, that's not what happened.

They snatched us away.

My sister Rebecca is older than me by all of 18 months. Me and her were bounced around for a bit, but eventually we got adopted.

I bet you're wondering how I came to be lying in a foster home bed, then — if I had already been adopted. A new foster home. One without a dad, which I was thankful for.

Whelp.

Turns out adoptions can be undone.

The family that had adopted me — Elton and Patricia Hayes — were abusive, and that's just putting it mildly. Me and my sister weren't even in kindergarten when they adopted us, so we were young. Young with a lot of baggage. And our bags were full of trauma.

Instead of getting me and my sister therapy to help us work through the trauma we had experienced, they compounded it by "disciplining" us. When I wet the bed, I would be spanked and humiliated.

That's right.

Instead of seeing that something was scaring me — preventing me from getting up and out of bed — I'd get whipped with a skinny belt. Most likely a purse strap.

It wasn't like I wanted to pee the bed. And even with their rule of no milk or any sort of beverage after dinner, I'd still manage to wet my bed.

I would be made to strip my bedding and hang it outside, and before bed the next day, I'd have to retrieve it from around the side of the house.

I was terrified of the dark.

I'd try to do the task as quickly as possible, my young mind thinking if I was quick, no harm would come to me.

So I'd quickly exit the house through the kitchen back door, run across the patio — making sure not to get close to the pool and fall in — and go to the side of the yard, which had no lighting whatsoever.

These antics were all for nothing, though.

My adoptive brother Jason — my adoptive family's biological son — would lay in wait for me outside in the bushes, just to scare me.

It worked every time. I was easy to scare.

Other times, when Jason was bored, he would body slam me to the floor.

Random, right?

Not so much.

See, Jason was into football, and he would simply be "playing" — even though I'd be somersaulted in the air, landing on the living room floor with the wind knocked out of me.

He yelled "tackle" first, so… duh, it was all in good fun.

The spankings weren't the worst, though.

These Christian parents — the ones the State felt were fit to care for me and my sister — would force us into ice baths as punishment. And when Patrica didn't feel like filling the tub with ice and cold water and holding mine or my sister's head under, she'd make us kneel on hard tile floors for hours with a paper bag over our heads.

Ensuring we were in pain and disoriented.

Me and my sister would try to whisper to each other, keep each other's minds off the pain — but if we were caught talking or peeking out from under the bag, we'd get more time.

Sometimes we spent the entire afternoon on our knees with bags over our heads.

I bet you're wondering who saved us from this torturous treatment. A friendly neighbor? A teacher?

None of the above.

They just got tired of us.

Turns out the State's return policy is open-ended.

So of course, my 15-year-old self was angry and confused.

I had been sexually abused by foster families I'd been placed in and mentally, emotionally, and physically abused by my adoptive family.

Families that the State certified and gave licenses to.

I was taken away from my mother because she had a drug problem — a victim of the '80s crack epidemic — but waking up in this bed, pushed against the wall to make room for the bunk beds on the other side of the room and the dresser with drawers that wanted to fall off the hinges every time you pulled them out, with mismatched sheets, a scratchy comforter, and a thin pillow, was upsetting.

Nothing was fair.

Call me ungrateful if you want.

I would've rather the State had minded their damn business and left me in my actual mother's care.

There was no way living with her, even on drugs, could have been any worse than any of the placements the State decided were in my best interest.

After the adoption was terminated, me and my sister were placed back into the system.

Wards of the State again.

Our first stop: a shelter.

Shelters didn't always have room, so once again, me and my sister were separated. I went through three different temporary placements until my social worker was able to find a placement for both of us together.

Promise House. A Christian-based group home.

The last family I was placed with had been Christians — the father was a pastor even, of a small home-based church — so being Christian didn't really hold the badge of high morality and integrity people thought it did. Anyone could be Christian.

Me and my sister got kicked out of this group home. My sister was the first to get the boot, though. I followed a few years later.

They said I had anger issues and needed a more therapeutic environment.

You see, in these types of settings — State-run homes or shelters — they didn't want to deal with an angry child who couldn't regulate their emotions.

I didn't know how to regulate my emotions because, while living with my adoptive parents, I wasn't allowed to have any.

Too hyper or wild? Spanked.

Made the wrong face while being spoken to? Spanked.

Didn't respond fast enough, react quick enough? Punished.

I had become like one of those beaten and abused dogs you see in the commercials with the sad music in the background. Skittish and afraid. I remember ducking or walking past either of them quickly just to avoid getting hit upside the head.

Going to the shelter changed me.

In the shelter, I saw girls coming in and out of the house as they pleased. Cursing and getting into arguments with staff members — their elders. Authoritative figures.

They were doing things that would've gotten me beat and sent to kneel in the corner with a bag over my head for hours. Except… they weren't getting beat.

As far as I could tell, they weren't getting consequences at all. Not any real ones.

Deciding they didn't want what was being offered for dinner wasn't an issue. They were given the option to make a sandwich or eat a bowl of cereal.

They weren't told to sit at the table until they finished their food.

This was my turning point. My Breaking Bad moment.

I'm way too old to remember the situation entirely, but basically, I had gotten upset about something in the shelter.

Being around those girls made me forget myself — and my learned well-mannered behavior — and I got up from the table without being excused.

I stomped down the hallway, each step full of attitude.

I went into the room assigned to me and slammed the door.

Once in the bedroom, I realized what I had done. I started to panic. Started questioning why I had just done all that.

My heart began to thump loudly in my chest.

I tried to calm my racing heart as I heard the footsteps of staff coming down the hall to my room.

I sat on the bed to await whatever my consequences might be.

The door opened.

"Nicole," she said my name with a stern voice. It didn't invoke any fear in me, though.

"Slamming doors will not be tolerated in this house. You understand?"

I nodded, still unsure of my fate — but not sensing any harm headed my way either.

"Now stand up."

I stood.

"I want you to open and shut this door properly. Ten times."

I obeyed.

I also learned something that day. Not the lesson she wanted me to learn but…

I had no real consequences. The staff couldn't exactly make me do anything I didn't want to do.

They didn't have any power. Not like my adoptive parents did.

I could get mad.

I could lash out.

So of course, being a child of 10 or 11, I went entirely too far at Promise House — with all the many feelings I had repressed.

I didn't have a middle ground.

I was either shy, timid, or full-on monster.

Promise House was actually in Peoria — the same city I had lived in with my adoptive parents after they moved from Oregon with us. Peoria, back then anyway, was the distant suburbs.

At Promise House, we were expected to attend church every week and sometimes even on Wednesdays. When bored, me and some of the other girls would walk to church by ourselves and attend Bible study. There were four horses on the property that we were tasked to feed and water, and on the weekends, we would all go trail riding. Every girl's house — no matter her background — ended up riding horses, including me and my sister.

We weren't allowed to listen to any music unless it was Christian or country music. Only those genres were considered to be "clean." So I loved me some Shania Twain, Reba McEntire, Tim McGraw.

When I was getting along with the other girls, we played a lot of card games: Uno, Skip-Bo, variations of Speed, War, Slap Jack — and we'd even try to do card tricks too. We played all the classic board games: Life, Candy Land, Monopoly (I actually hated that game — it lasted too long), and Mancala.

On weekends, when we weren't horseback riding or it was a holiday, we spent a lot of time taking turns playing Tetris and trying to beat each other's high scores. Brick Attack was another household favorite. At some point, we got a Sega Genesis, and we'd take turns playing Sonic, Toy Story, and The Lion King. I was no good at video games, though — I'd end up playing one round and watching the rest of the time. Or just watching TV.

Being a Christian home, there were a lot of things we could not watch, actually. King of the Hill, Family Guy, The Simpsons, and SpongeBob were all no-gos. Instead, we watched VHS Disney tapes — didn't have a Blu-ray player yet — and shows like 7th Heaven, Touched by an Angel, and One Saturday Morning cartoons.

All of these games and activities were things I had never seen played or experienced while I'd been adopted by the Hayeses or placed in foster homes or shelters.

Actually, I didn't even know how to read until I got to the Promise House group home. My adoptive family had been too busy homeschooling their two older sons, so although we were all homeschooled, me and my sister just tried to stay out of the way.

I entered the fifth grade not knowing anything. Thankfully, living in the distant suburbs of Peoria meant we had great teachers. Instead of attending class, I was given a private tutor. I'd show up to the school, go to my first-period homeroom, and then I'd spend the rest of the school day with my tutor in a small room.

I don't know how long it actually took me to learn how to read, but I met with that old man every day until I did.

Oddly enough, he didn't tutor me in math — which I also did not know. The teachers loved giving timed multiplication tests, which gave me so much anxiety because I was trying to do multiplication by doing addition multiple times.

And if you're thinking, "Yeah, that's what multiplication is"—I mean, I was literally making a bunch of marks on my paper and then counting them.

Very tedious.

Very slow.

Simply learning to read wasn't enough to make me feel like I was even close to on level with the other kids.

I tried sitting in the back of the class a lot because I didn't know what was going on. I didn't know what was going on because I was so far behind — and I couldn't even see the board.

I should've been sitting in the very front of the class, but I felt stupid. I felt insecure. And so the back is where I felt safe.

Looking back, Promise House actually had a lot to offer. And had I not been so messed up and angry, a lot of the other things that happened in my life probably wouldn't have happened.

The staff weren't actually terrible. I remember when I got chickenpox, Danny took me home to her house. Another staff member, Melissa, would let us go to her house and swim in her pool.

Promise House is the classic: It's not you. It's me.

It wasn't them. It was me.

I was just coming into my freedom of emotions.

If I got upset, I was yelling — something I had never been allowed to do before. I was refusing to do things I didn't want to do, because no one could make me. I was hitting others because no one could hit me back — or at least they weren't allowed or supposed to. I was kicking holes in walls because they'd fix it and simply tell me not to do it again.

My behavior, despite their niceness, was poor.

The group decided they wanted to go on vacation and take a trip to Disneyland. I was the one who didn't get to go. Since the entire house was leaving, I was sent away for the vacation period to a respite home — where I was sad and upset. When they returned and I was allowed to go back to the group home, the girls were excited, showing pictures of the time they had, talking about "remember this" and "remember that," and I raged even more.

Excluding me was cruel — and I was gonna let them know exactly how I felt.

I slapped Nikki in the face, and I poured green paint in Melissa's hair.

They called the police on me. And while I waited for the police to show up, I was actually scared. The police did finally come. We sat down at the kitchen table and had a chat.

A consequence for my poor behavior.

I was mad at my caseworker too. So, whenever she would come to the group home to visit, I was disrespectful — merely on principle. The State would always be my enemy. I went through a few different caseworkers, and each one I made sure to let know they were a bitch.

After the police tactic failed, I was sent to Scared Straight.

Yeah — my 12-year-old self actually went to prison for the day.

We were yelled at a bit, which was very intense and made me sad, of course, because I'd been yelled at a lot and intimidated a lot by my former adoptive parents. The entire event was scary — until we got to the men's unit.

Oddly enough, they weren't scary.

When I was in the girls' unit, they were screaming and threatening bodily harm, banging on the walls of their cells. The men didn't do any of that. Actually, they just talked. We sat around in a large circle and ate lunch with them. They seemed to be full of regret. One told me he had a daughter my age, but he never got to see her outside of photos.

The women were like animals.

But the men — I actually felt bad for.

Talking to them, seeing how sad, miserable, and upset they were with a life of failure and disappointment — that was more impactful than having women scream and bang on bars.

I felt like… if these big, strong, gang-banger criminal men could feel regret, longing, suffering, hatred for where they were — then this place was really nowhere I wanted to be.

Of course, out of sight, out of mind though.

My behavior at the group home didn't exactly change, so I was sent to Boot Camp.

While at Boot Camp, I of course behaved. Not immediately — I did a few push-ups due to disrespect — but then I got tired of doing push-ups, so I shut my mouth.

But of course, when I got back to the group home, I literally had no real consequences. Again. I misbehaved again, and that was it.

They had tried everything.

I was being kicked out of the group home.

My sister hadn't done nearly as much as I had, and she'd been kicked out before me because she was constantly bullying me. So they just decided it was actually better to keep us separated.

The group home I was placed in was a behavioral health residential treatment facility. I was no longer in Peoria — instead, I was in Tempe. The neighborhood and house were nice, although it wasn't a ranch-style home in the distant suburbs with horses in the backyard. It was a two-story home in the suburbs, with a neighborhood park and a school within walking distance.

Apart from the girls in the home trying to cut themselves, the house was pretty uneventful.

I was back to my former self — the scared, quiet kid, watching in the background, because these girls were not my age and I was completely out of my element.

I didn't fight with any of the girls at this placement. Actually, I don't think any of the girls fought with each other either. There were girls I didn't care for, or didn't want to be around.

I was the youngest at the house and the only girl attending Kyrene Middle School from the group home. I would ride the bus to school and walk by myself every morning, alone, to and from it.

I didn't mind all the solitude.

I was used to it. The last school I'd been at was Frontier, and it was probably the most involved when it came to socializing on the playground and just in general. I actually played jump rope at recess with some of the other kids. However, I never participated in PE or sports — and that was more or less the same at all my other schools. I'd sit against the wall at recess by myself. At the swings by myself.

So, it was no different at this new school — Kyrene Middle School.

I would take my Walkman in my backpack, listen to it while I was on the bus, get off the bus, and attend classes. I was shy. I was beyond shy. I wanted invisible. Being in a group home was embarrassing for me. I felt like everyone knew — and I didn't want them to know. I was the kid with no parents.

I was the kid who could never go on a field trip because I didn't have money.

I was the kid who couldn't buy snacks at lunch because I didn't have money.

I didn't participate in PE — partly because I had asthma.

And while at Frontier Elementary, back at Promise House, there were times I thought I was legit going to die. I was pleading and bargaining with God to save my life, promising that I would behave if He did.

The other reason I didn't participate in PE was because I never wanted to dress out for it. It was cold in the mornings, and I was also not comfortable undressing in the locker rooms. And while there were three stalls, they were typically occupied. So, I just didn't participate. Honestly, I didn't believe anybody wanted me on their teams when we played sports anyhow. No one actually tried to befriend me.

At lunch, I'd get my food and immediately go to the restrooms. I'd head into a stall, eat my lunch, and sit in the bathroom until I heard the bell ring signaling lunch had ended.

Then I'd walk to the bus, take an empty seat, pull out my radio Walkman, and listen to one of my favorite afterschool shows.

3:30 Dirty. I looked forward to listening to it in the afternoon — and phone scams in the morning.

Once home, we'd have therapy.

I don't ever remember doing homework. Probably because I didn't do any. But I do remember group therapy — and being prescribed Ritalin.

I hated group therapy. The dining room was also the therapy room, and therapy always seemed to be arts and crafts or workbook exercises. Like I said, my memory is pretty bad. I blocked out a lot. But one therapy session I do remember clearly — this guy came in and decided our workbook exercise should be writing our own obituary.

Now, the other girls were high schoolers, bearing age, but I was an eighth grader — writing an obituary. I hardly even knew what an obituary was.

Reflecting back now, I can't help but wonder… why would anyone in their right mind have suicidal girls write an obituary?

That's pretty close to the kind of letters written just before a permanent act is taken.

This man would come in, lead a discussion, then give us these tasks to complete.

I hated living at this house.

Sure, it was quiet, and there was no drama or fights with the other girls — but it had its own kind of chaos. The kind of chaos where every night before bed, I was given a small pink pill to take. And every morning before school, I was given that pink pill again.

Everybody in the home was given some sort of pill.

We were all medicated. For all different reasons.

Based on my last group home, I was said to be defiant and to have Attention Deficit Disorder. I'm not sure what medication the other girls were taking. I just know that, like mine, it didn't work — because it didn't stop the girls from sneaking razor blades from shavers and cutting their thighs and arms any chance they got.

I used to cheek my meds — which is why, for me, they didn't work. They couldn't work. I wasn't taking them.

I find it hilarious that staff and questionable therapists believed the medication was working.

I had such a large stockpile of Ritalin, I was constantly moving it to different hiding places because I was afraid of getting caught and being put on restriction. Eventually, on my walk home from the bus stop, I threw the entire stash into the neighbor's rosebush.

I didn't belong in a place like this.

I had been angry, sure — but my anger was at the world. At the system I was placed into. I hated Child Protective Services. I hated everyone affiliated.

These girls, however…

They hated themselves.

Foster homes were sketchy and unpredictable — a gamble.

One I was willing to take, though. Because after six months of being on my best behavior, my caseworker came to let me know I'd be leaving the group home and placed with a foster family.

It had been a long time since I'd lived in an actual home setting. In a way, I was looking forward to it.

I didn't want to feel like the kid at school with no parents anymore.

I was embarrassed having staff listed as my legal guardian.

My caseworker picked me up and took me to meet the first foster family. I packed a bag with enough clothes for the weekend, and we headed somewhere west.

The neighborhood this home was in looked familiar — similar to the one I'd just left — but it was more active. Kids were outside, throwing footballs and riding bikes in the street. It felt… hopeful at first glance.

When I walked inside, the home was large and clean. Children were everywhere — out back, at the barstools in the kitchen, in the living room, in the bedrooms. It was a Black family, with both boys and girls in the home. The parents seemed friendly… but strict.

Something about that scared me.

My adoptive parents had been friendly at first glance too — Christian and strict. On some level, subconsciously, I imagine that's why I decided not to choose them. That, and the number of children already living there. I had no clue whether any of the kids were their biological children or if all were foster placements. Either way, I wasn't interested in being one of eight kids calling them "Mom" and "Dad."

A few weeks passed, and I was visiting the next foster home for a couple of days. This home was nothing like any of the places I remembered living in before.

The homes weren't two-stories. There were no large backyards, no horses, no nice cars, no garages. Actually, when we pulled up, I saw cars sitting on the lawn, cars parked on the street, in carports, in driveways.

City buses. Freeways. Motels within walking distance.

I was in Maryvale.

51st Ave and McDowell.

Cheap motels. Truck stops. Waffle House. A barbershop.

The 99-cent store. Domino's Pizza. Jiffy Lube.

I had never lived in walking distance to a fast-food restaurant, hotel, or freeway in all of my thirteen years.

These weren't even places I'd driven past before — not on any field trip, outing, or transport.

So why had I agreed to live at this foster home, huh?

The woman was Black. She seemed young and vibrant. Her hair was done nice. She had on good makeup. And most of all — there were no boys in the house. She was unmarried and, from what my young mind could gather, single.

So here I was. Lying in a twin-sized bed with mismatched sheets, in the dimly lit, cluttered, four-bedroom rental home of my new foster mother — Vanity Vaughn, a Mary Kay consultant — smack in the middle of the poverty-stricken neighborhood of Maryvale.

The classic, stereotypical ghetto of the 90s.

Streets full of pimps and their tricks. Gang members and petty criminals running wild. Drug dealers. Drug users.

My first experience with the harshness of this new neighborhood happened after I got off the city bus — the same one I rode back and forth from school, like many other high schoolers in the area.

I stepped off the bus and started walking the few blocks home when a car pulled up alongside me.

"Do you need a ride?" the male driver asked.

"No, I just live up the street."

He drove off.

Not even a minute later, I nearly jumped off the sidewalk when another driver honked and yelled something at me from his car.

This was my new home.

And I had no guidance.

No one helping me navigate this completely foreign and chaotic territory I'd suddenly been dropped into.

It was only a matter of time.

So, yeah. I was angry.

The state had taken me away from my drug-addicted mother and placed me in various homes — only to let me be adopted by abusive parents. And when that fell apart, I was displaced again, moved all the way from Oregon to Arizona, bounced around a new state-run system, only to end up in a neighborhood filled with people just like the mother they claimed to be saving me from.

And I became a product of my environment.

A statistic.

Fifteen and pregnant.

Before it was even cool.

Before it was reality TV worthy.

How's The Baby?

"I'm grabbing my keys and heading to the car. Don't forget to grab the drink out of the fridge," Vanity said, standing in the doorway of my room. She was dressed like she was headed to dinner or a date. She always dressed this way, though—even when checking the mailbox. A fresh weave, caked-on makeup, heels, and skin-tight clothes to show off her curves.

"You never know who will see you," she would say.

I rolled out of bed and quickly changed out of the sweatpants and t-shirt I slept in, throwing on a clean pair of sweats and a large white t-shirt. I scanned the room for my sneakers but didn't see them, so I checked under the bed. They ended up there by accident more times than I liked to admit. You'd think I'd learn my lesson and take them off closer to the door—but nope.

Not wanting to bend down, I went into the closet and slipped on a pair of flip-flops. All this movement jostled my belly, and I started to feel pressure on my bladder. I sighed out loud to myself, annoyed with how often I needed to pee lately. I decided to hold it, though, because the doctor's office staff would be ready to shove a cup in my hand anyway.

I walked down the hall, passing the dining room table. It was atrocious. No one could eat there unless the outdated magazines, old mail, and other random articles were meant to serve as placemats.

I opened the fridge. It was full of condiments, leftover takeout, a jug of water, a few cans of soda, and the unnaturally bright red drink given to me at my last OBGYN appointment.

I took the 8 oz. bottle of liquid sugar from the fridge and let the door swing shut. Walking to the front door, I read the tag attached to the bottle cap:

Drink the Oral Glucose Tolerance Beverage within 5 minutes, 30 minutes before your appointment. Your blood must be drawn precisely one hour after you have completed the beverage. Upon arrival, notify the front desk when you finished your drink. Do not eat or drink until after your blood is drawn.

"Well, come on!" Vanity yelled out the window of her car, as if being on time was suddenly important to her. "You got your drink?"

I lifted the bottle to show her I had it and got into the back seat.

"Nicole, stop playing with the drink and drink it," Vanity said, looking at me through the mirror.

I opened the bottle and took the smallest of sips. I gagged.

"I can't do this. This is gross."

"Don't sip it—down the entire bottle."

I took a large gulp and started sputtering. "Oh my God, this is the nastiest thing I've ever drank."

"Stop… I know it's not that bad."

I took another gulp. "This is toxic."

A few more forced gulps and swallows and I finished the drink.

***

I took my time walking up the path to the doctor's office, making Vanity hold the door for me. The office was elegant, with deep dark green chairs and small end tables with magazines. The floors were polished, and the walls had quotes and flowery images.

Under any other circumstance, I might have actually liked coming to this office. Like if I wasn't pregnant and people weren't staring at me like I was the first teen to ever be in this predicament. Let an adult tell it, being 15 and pregnant is right up there with murder. How dare I have had sex. That's an act reserved for married adults in committed, loving relationships. To do it in any other order is simply promiscuous and sinful.

I imagine that's why Vanity, the devoted Christian she is, is working hard to find her fifth husband.

I followed behind Vanity as she strutted across the room to the front desk, her heels clicking and clacking against the tile.

"Hi, how may I help you?" the front desk clerk asked with a smile.

"We have a 9:30. This is Nicole," Vanity replied, shoving her right thumb in my direction.

"Okay," the front desk clerk said, looking at her computer. "When did she finish the drink?"

"About 9 o'clock."

"Great," the woman said, still smiling as she handed Vanity a clipboard. "Look over the information and tell me if anything has changed—address or insurance."

Vanity gave the clipboard a quick glance and handed it back. "No changes."

"Okay, thank you. Have a seat, and the doctor will call you shortly."

I sat against the wall in the back, picked up a magazine, and started flipping through pictures, only stopping to read catchy headlines and check my horoscope. I didn't believe the writer of the horoscope had any insight into my life—or anyone else's—but I liked reading positive things attributed to myself. A little personal affirmation.

"Nicole Hayes!" a nurse in a blue lab coat called.

I followed her back through the double doors, with Vanity at my heels.

"Go ahead and pee in this cup, and then we'll get your weight."

I took the cup, suddenly reminded of how badly I had needed to pee since the car ride over.

The nurse took my weight and walked us back to a small room. I sat on the examination table and Vanity sat in a chair next to me.

"A lab tech will be in shortly to take your blood," said the nurse as she walked out of the room.

I looked away as the tech drew my blood. It wasn't that I minded the blood—I watched the vials fill up—but I couldn't watch the needle go in or I'd tense up. The lab tech gave me a band-aid and left. Me and Vanity were left to sit in awkward silence until the doctor came in.

Knock, knock.

"Hi Nicole, looks like you're a little over 28 weeks. How are you feeling?"

"Fine."

What else could I really say anyway? I was miserable. And I hated coming to these appointments for a baby I had been trying hard not to get emotionally attached to, especially since the state had made it abundantly clear that, as a child, I was too young to raise one.

And I wouldn't even know how to put that into words—simply or otherwise. And what could she do anyway?

Give me a sad smile.

Say: I'm sure he'll go to a good, loving family.

Yes, that's what they want you to believe. But here I am—with a lifetime of trauma and no loving family.

Except my unborn family.

The one I have to give up.

And man-crazed Vanity, looking for a check and her next husband.

"Have you started to feel the baby move?" the doctor asks, placing her hand on my belly.

"We're going to listen to the heartbeat," she continues, lifting up my shirt.

She squeezes the cold blue gel onto my stomach and presses the wand against it.

A loud swooshing fills the room—like crashing waves or a roaring ocean.

"Is that the heartbeat?" I ask. Then mentally kick myself.

It doesn't matter. I don't want to get attached to the idea of a life I'll never have.

This will not be my baby. This will not be my family.

I have to remind myself.

When I first learned I was pregnant, I tried to hide it.

I just knew my caseworker would move me back into a group home, and my child would automatically become a ward of the state—right along with me.

Both of us: property of the system.

Our futures left to caseworkers and state employees.

I despised the Department of Child Safety. They never kept me safe.

But no one questioned them. The court system stands firmly behind their decisions.

Because of course—they know what's best.

They read a textbook.

"Yes," the doctor says, smiling. "A good strong heartbeat."

I glance at Vanity. She seems excited—like she's catching baby fever.

But it doesn't make sense. She made it clear she wasn't licensed to have a baby in her home.

So why the glow?

Just last week, we both sat at a large wooden table at the CPS office with my caseworker, her supervisor, and two women I had never seen before.

I learned they were my guardian ad litem and my CASA.

Apparently, I'd always had a guardian ad litem—I just didn't know it until that meeting.

Of course, they all claimed to have my best interest at heart.

They knew what was best for a foster girl like me.

I had heard enough of them talking about me like I wasn't even in the room, so I left.

I wandered the halls. I don't even know how the meeting ended.

All I know is that in the days that followed, my CASA presented me with a family looking to adopt my child.

Not one adult asked how I got pregnant.

I mean, sure—they technically knew how, but no one asked who.

No one asked who had gotten me pregnant. Who the father was.

No one cared.

I don't even think Vanity was questioned.

She was my guardian—how did I get pregnant on her watch?

It was just assumed: I was a bad, promiscuous child who didn't listen.

That's how I got pregnant.

Their only concern was how to get their hands on my unborn child—and how "lovely" the family was that they had in mind.

My CASA wasn't the only one.

Another woman—a "special friend"—invited me to a luncheon.

After feeding me and buttering me up, she presented her recommended family for adoption too.

It was like being pitched to.

Basically, a newborn baby is better than currency.

People want babies.

They want them badly enough that they are more than willing—excited, even—to build a family from the crisis and suffering of others.

A teen mother with no support.

Any mother with no support, really.

The family-less, the barren, the gays, the religious—all of them see an opportunity to build a family.

Or sell your child.

Through the private or state adoption system.

The state would rather label you unfit and snatch the child away than coach and guide the mother.

If someone had helped my mother, rather than profiting from her crisis, I might not be in this doctor's office right now—laying on my back, listening to the heartbeat of a child I'll never get to raise.

The doctor hands me a warm towel to wipe the gel from my swollen belly.

"Thank you," I say, grabbing it.

"Your lab results came back," she adds. "Your iron levels have improved significantly. That's good. It's very important—low levels can lead to serious health issues, and we want to avoid that."

"Yes, I've been drinking the tea daily," I say.

"Well that's just great! Do you have any questions or concerns for me?" the doctor asks while charting her notes.

"No," I say, standing up.

"Alright, we'll see you in about four weeks. Schedule your appointment up front."

***

I sit in the back seat, same as I did on the way to the doctor's office, and stretch the seatbelt across my lap before pulling my legs up onto the seat.

"I have a married daughter living across town," Vanity says, eyeing me in the mirror. "She and her husband don't have any children."

Her too, huh? I think to myself. Every single adult in my life is set on rehoming my unborn child like a puppy in a shelter.

"Sure. I'll speak with your daughter," I say flatly. "Are you taking me to school?"

"That was the plan. That's kind of why I made your appointment early."

"After drinking that drink, I really don't feel well," I lie.

Physically, I'm fine. I just hate being the pregnant girl on campus.

"Nicole," she says in a stern voice, locking eyes with me in the rearview mirror—trying to figure out if I'm full of shit.

"What?" I whine. "My stomach really is upset. That drink was pure sugar." I'm really trying to sell this lie.

After the appointment and now the conversation about her daughter, I have zero desire to squeeze myself into one of those awful desks at school. Why is the seat attached? It's like a built-in judgment. You literally have to be slim to fit into a school desk, and with my pregnancy nearing the end, I'm anything but slim.

And don't even get me started on health class.

Seriously—why has no one thought to change my schedule and remove me from this class? It says so much about the brainless education system we're in. I'm the pregnant girl being forced to watch videos of hippies preach about abstinence and safe sex.

How the safest sex is no sex at all.

How condoms protect against STDs, infections, and—wait for it—pregnancy.

I sit there as a real-life example of what not to do.

Nicole: Exhibit A.

My unfortunate, unplanned pregnancy.

You know what they should be teaching?

How to avoid pimps and predators in crime-ridden neighborhoods.

Maybe a unit on how not to be a rape victim—or how to escape one.

Where was that class?

We had D.A.R.E.—teaching kids to say no to drugs—but nothing about sexual abuse.

Apparently, safe sex is only a concern for the consenting.

Dance class isn't any better. I picked it because it's creative and seemed like an easy A. I mean, how do you even fail dance?

Turns out, it's actually pretty easy when your teacher docks points for being late to every class.

Maybe my dance instructor thinks she's being progressive by including me, but she's actually making my life harder.

Expecting a heavily pregnant teenager to climb two flights of stairs to the locker room, change clothes, and make it to the stretch mat before the bell rings?

Yeah… not helpful.

"Okay, Nicole," Vanity finally says, giving me another glance. "We'll pretend you're sick today."

I let out a sigh of relief and sink back into the seat, staring out the window as we pass houses and businesses on our way to the freeway.

Not My Baby

By the time we make it back home, my stomach feels like it's touching my back. I know with being pregnant that's impossible, but I'm starving. I couldn't eat anything before the glucose test—the doctors didn't want the food to throw off the results.

Vanity heads in the opposite direction down the hall to her bedroom. I go straight to the kitchen and search the pantry for a packet of instant chicken noodles. Grabbing two, I start looking for a clean pot. I know the odds are slim because no one really does dishes in this house. We just wash whatever we need, use it, and then toss it right back into the sink for next time.

By we, I mean Vanity, her two older daughters Tashia and Kianna, and another foster daughter, Shetorae. Shetorae showed up a couple months after I'd already been placed with Vanity. Thankfully, she didn't stay long. She was a certified pathological liar that I could hardly stand to be around.

Neither of Vanity's biological daughters were trying to deal with another sibling, let alone a foster one. Both of them kept to themselves—Kianna more than her older sister, Tashia. Tashia would speak to me every once in a while— the occasional, "What's up, Nicole?"—but Kianna wouldn't say a word to me unless she had to. And we went to the same school.

They also ate all their meals in their rooms, so I never actually saw them eat or what they ate. Just knew they did, based on the dishes in the sink—and the fact that they were still alive.

I find a small pot in the sink that'll work and squirt a few drops of liquid soap directly into it. I hate using raggedy sponges or the ones with dried food caked onto the scrub side, so I just turn on the water and use my hand to move the soap around. Once there's enough suds to call it clean, I rinse it out and fill it with water to boil.

The noodles are supposed to cook for 3 minutes, but I don't time it. I stir them around and just eyeball the softness. When they look ready, I drain most of the water, mix in the seasoning packets, and pour the contents into a paper bowl.

Vanity doesn't like me eating in the living room, but the dining table is basically a storage unit at this point—stacks of branded makeup magazines, unopened product boxes, and mail both old and new.

I carry my bowl to the living room and grab the remote. I've become obsessed with this show where women don't know they're pregnant until they go into labor. Being more than halfway through my pregnancy, all I can really think about is giving birth. The idea of the pain my body will have to go through terrifies me. But watching this show gives me strength, weirdly. Like, if those women can give birth at a campground, in a bathtub, or even on a toilet—alone—I can handle a hospital birth.

"Nicole!" Vanity yells from her bedroom. Her favorite pastime: not getting up.

"Yes?"

"Come here."

I grab my empty paper bowl and slowly rise from where I'm sitting on the living room floor, my back against the sofa. Whatever she wants, it's not urgent. She loves to call my name, have me come all the way to her room, and then ask me to fetch something she could've easily gotten herself.

Hovering in her doorway, I see she has the cordless phone pressed to her ear.

"Sit down," she says, patting the bed.

I sit on the edge of her king-sized bed, which is so high my feet dangle above the ground. Her blackout shades make the room feel darker than it should, and I start to feel a little claustrophobic from all the clutter. The entire right wall is taken up by two dressers, and on the left is a bookcase filled with everything but books. The wall opposite her bed has a giant cabinet-style TV stand, crammed with VHS tapes and DVDs, and on top sits a flat-screen tube TV. The walking space in her room is narrow and honestly dangerous.

"I have my daughter Vivian on the phone," she says, switching it to speaker. "She and her husband James don't have any children and have been married for five years," she continues. "They've been wanting to adopt."

"Hi, Nicole. Can you hear me?"

"Yeah," I say, getting up to sit closer to Vanity and the receiver.

"My mother was telling me about your situation, and we would love to help—you being family and all."

Vanity interrupts to chime in, "If you let my daughter Vivian adopt your son, you'll know where he lives. You'll be able to see him whenever you want."

I contemplate her words. My biggest fear is losing the closest thing I have to family. My baby going into the system—or worse, giving birth and never seeing him again. I rub my belly as I feel my child kick. I know I don't have many options. Somebody other than me is going to raise my baby. They'll gain a child and build their family from my crisis. I won't get to enjoy the silver lining of my own trauma—the child that was conceived. My child…

"I'll be able to see him whenever I want?" I ask, having recently learned I'd be having a boy.

"Whenever you want," Vanity says, placing her heavily jeweled hand on my knee. "You're my foster daughter. You're part of our family."

"I know we haven't met yet, sweetie, so if you need more time, that's fine," Vivian adds gently.

"I don't know," I say, using my favorite verbal filler.

No one speaks. I sit in the quiet, thinking about my options and the families that have come to me so far with offers to adopt my son. All of them offering a two-parent household and a better life—a life a 15-year-old foster girl can't give. And why would I, they say. I have my whole life ahead of me. What about college?

But Vanity and her daughter aren't saying all that. They aren't trying to whisk my son away. They want to give me the chance to still be part of his life.

"I don't need more time. You and your husband can adopt my baby," I say quietly. I have to pick a family, and while I don't really know Vivian, she is Vanity's daughter.

Vanity is squeezing my knee firmly now, clearly unable to contain her excitement.

"Really?" Vivian says, her voice trembling. "We've been wanting to start a family, and this would mean so much to me."

She sounds like she's about to cry, which makes me uncomfortable. I'm not agreeing out of the kindness of my heart. I don't want to give my baby away. This is not an exciting time for me.

"We should plan a baby shower," Vanity exclaims, clapping her hands together.

"Yes! When's your due date? I'd want to have the house ready," Vivian says.

"July 6th."

"So roughly twelve weeks to go."

"That's more than enough time to plan something," Vanity says.

I get up from the foot of the bed and start toward the door.

"Wait—do we know who the father is? Will he object to the adoption?"

I turn back and sit down on the bed again. "No, I'm not exactly sure who the father is. I wasn't tracking my periods or really paying attention to when I got pregnant."

I had actually been walking home with one of my friends and neighbors when, out of nowhere, I blurted out that I thought I was pregnant. I didn't even know how or why. There weren't any tell-tale signs. I just felt pregnant.

"I never took the time to try and backtrack or work out a timeline," I say.

Vanity is staring at me with judgment, and Vivian lets out a soft, "Oh," followed by silence.

I don't feel like explaining to them that the father could be my friend Laquanna's brother. That whenever I went over to her house and she wasn't paying attention, her brother would be chatting me up. That he invited me back over once to braid his hair and spent the entire time reaching around, trying to feel me up. That I didn't really mind the attention and followed him back to his room. There's no real point in mentioning that I lost a friend just to later find out he's not even the father. Instead, it's the random older guy from New York I met at a party—the one who invited me into the bathroom.

He'd seemed especially nice, especially after what had happened minutes earlier when my foster sister Shetora lured me into a room, locked the door, or maybe even held it from the outside while some man tried to take my clothes off. Thankfully, he gave up fighting with me and I left the room upset—only to be approached by the nice man from New York.

I had no desire to go into any of that.

"Yeah," I say in a low voice, mostly to myself. I get up from the bed for the second time and walk to my room to lie down.

***

I guess there's such a thing as pregnancy insomnia, which I must have, because I cannot get to sleep for the life of me. I feel wide awake, and my mind just won't rest. I reach for the worn paperback on my nightstand—The Girl with the Silver Eyes—to try and distract myself, but I'm just staring at the words, not really comprehending anything I read.

The talk with Vanity and Vivian has me feeling like I finally have a solid plan. I can tell my social worker at our next meeting that a family plan for my unborn child has been created. I should feel relief—the fate of my child is no longer in limbo, and my baby doesn't have to grow up not knowing who I am.

Still, I can't stop wondering how this open adoption is actually going to work. Will my baby call us both Mom? Will I play the role of the aunt? I've heard of this sort of thing before—a child growing up alongside his mother and not learning the truth until much later. What's a good age to tell a child that his "aunt" is really his birth mother, who had him young?

I replay the conversation I had with Vivian and Vanity, not sure why I hadn't asked more questions. It's not like I didn't have any—I just hadn't thought of them in the moment. And now the moment feels gone.

Quite literally, the moment was gone. The phone call was over, and I was back in my bed, wide awake.

The idea of getting up crossed my mind—maybe I could check if I had any new messages on MySpace or BlackPlanet. But the thought of waiting for AOL dial-up to connect felt like too much work for such a small distraction. I sigh and let my hand drift back to The Girl with the Silver Eyes, flipping through the pages without even trying to read now, as my thoughts continue to spiral.

How would I even bring it up again? Vanity did say I was family, and Vivian seemed to feel the same, despite knowing little about me. I don't know when my thoughts turned into dreams, but the next thing I know, I'm being woken up for school.

Thankfully, it's the last week. I don't know what my grades are, but I'm sure they're not passing. I'm definitely failing math, biology, and dance—which only leaves health, history, and English.

Math was just way too confusing, with all the different formulas and then different steps for each formula. Somehow, you were just supposed to look at a problem and know the formula from memory and solve it. I guess pass or fail doesn't matter. I knew from an older girl I was in a group home with that as long as you had an 80% attendance rate, they would move you up a grade—because you were presented with the material.

No child left behind.

Her Baby Shower

I couldn't fit into my low-rise jeans anymore with the way my belly kept growing, and I didn't want to wear my new normal attire of sweatpants and a large T-shirt, so I searched the closet for a nice summer dress. I ended up finding a long-sleeve V-neck baby doll dress that flared out just right to accent my baby bump.

"That's a nice dress," Vanity said, standing in my doorway. She was dressed in a leopard print blouse and blue jeans so tight they could've been sewn on. Her usual ensemble—makeup, jewelry on her hands, arms, neck, and ears—topped off with heels, of course.

"Don't take too long. I'll be in the car," she added before disappearing.

I went to my dresser and grabbed the bottle of lotion, quickly lathering it on my arms and legs, then slipped my feet into the 99-cent store flip-flops I'd bought with the handful of pennies and nickels Vanity had won playing the penny slots at the casino. I headed out to the car.

As we pulled up to Vanity's daughter Vivian's house, I saw a long line of cars parked alongside her home and on the opposite side of the street where there was a neighborhood park. Judging by how many cars and people were already gathered, I wondered what time the baby shower had actually started. There was no way they had all just arrived. Adults stood and sat on benches under the covered patio. Large balloons were tied to Vivian's mailbox and a few tables at the park. Coolers full of beers, sodas, and water sat at the ends of two long rows of picnic tables. Homemade baked goods were displayed on one table, and another held hot dogs, hamburgers, and hot links.

A few middle-aged men—relatives or friends, I had no way of knowing— were smoking a blunt. Before high school, I hadn't even known what a blunt was. I learned at a house party I went to with two girls from school I don't really talk to anymore.

They'd left me alone to mingle, so I sat at the kitchen counter, looking at what I thought were the fallen leaves of a dried-up plant. I guess I had been looking at a dried-up plant—just not the kind I thought. I had no idea the stuff I was crushing and playing with in my hand had any value. Bored, I opened my palm and swept the pieces off the counter onto the floor.

A guy I hadn't even noticed watching me jumped up. "Why are you throwing the weed on the floor?" he demanded.

Between puffs, they'd taken turns freestyle rapping, having an impromptu battle. I tried to pay attention, but I didn't understand all the references and slang. I just watched, entertained by the performance.

Back at the park, I saw Vanity making her way toward me.

"Here's my foster daughter, Nicole," she said, grabbing my hand and leading me toward a table. "This is my daughter Vivian."

"Hi," I said, doing a quick look around the table. I hated being put on the spot like this—standing beside Vanity like a puppy in a mall window.

"It's such a nice thing you're doing for Vivian," a woman said, smiling at me. "Vivian and James have been trying for a while."

I wondered what she'd told these women, because they were acting like I was some hired surrogate donating my body and time—rather than a teenage foster girl the state wouldn't let raise her own baby.

"Bless your heart," another woman added. "What you're doing really is amazing."

Vivian's face winced at their words. I imagined it was as hard for her as it was for me. This was weird. I was the girl having the baby, after all—the baby she had been trying for and couldn't have.

Why she decided to have a baby shower in a situation like this is beyond me. She could've just waited—gone shopping after the baby was born and told people she adopted a newborn. But no, she wanted the full show.

"Well, go on and get some food," Vanity says.

As starving as I am, I feel awkward mingling around people I don't know. People who stare at me and my protruding belly instead of speaking.

"I don't know what they have," I say, hoping Vanity will get up and walk with me to the food table so I don't have to do it alone.

"Nicole, just go and grab something," she says, waving her hand lazily toward the picnic tables. "James is putting some hot links on the grill now."

I glance across the way and see a tall, rather obese man—so that's Vivian's husband, James.

Hearing his name, he turns, and when he spots me, his face lights up. He puts down the tongs he was using to flip the links and walks straight toward me.

"It's so nice to meet you," he says, grabbing my hand before I have a chance to react. "I can't thank you enough for allowing us to adopt your child."

I snatch my hand back. Thankfully, he doesn't seem to notice. He probably thinks I'm just being shy, not that I hate unnecessary touching.

When I focus on him again, I see that his eyes are welling up with tears.

I'm not great with my own emotions to begin with, and now this man I just met is dumping his on me.

"I've just always wanted a child," his voice cracks. "We've been trying for years." He wipes his eyes. "I'm just so happy you picked us. Can I feel the baby?"

He places his hand on my belly before I can object. He seems truly overwhelmed, lost in the moment, and so I fight the urge to pull away.

It's annoying how adults feel like they have access to a pregnant woman's body just because there's a baby inside. Mostly, it's women who do it—walking up and touching my belly like I'm public property. And because they're always polite about it, I never say anything.

"And the baby's a boy, right?"

I nod.

"I've always loved the idea of having a son."

I smile, because I don't know what else to do. I'm exhausted by all of this. The small talk. The expectations. The pretending.

"I can't thank you enough," he says again, stepping closer with his arms out like he's about to hug me.

I take a step back before he can.

"You're welcome," I say quickly, turning to look for Vanity.

She's no longer at the table with Vivian. Instead, she's over by the patio, talking to two women about the new makeup products she just received.

"I'm tired. Can I go sit in the car?" I ask, holding out my hand for the keys.

Holding It In

I felt like a third wheel as Vanity and her best friend walked the downtown streets of the Fourth of July block party. Fireworks had never been that exciting to me. It was the same thing every year — if it weren't for the food trucks, art vendors, and live bands, I would have just walked back to the car and waited for Vanity.

Lately, she'd been making a point to drag me along to outings I had no interest in. It was her weak attempt to keep me out of trouble. Weak because anytime she had plans to meet up with Stanley or whichever other married man she was trying to lure, she had no issue leaving me behind to fend for myself.

In silent protest, I lagged behind while she chatted it up with her best friend. With nothing better to do, I tuned into their conversation.

By the time the fireworks show ended, most of the vendors had already packed up. Walking through the crowd of people desperate to reach their cars, I got bumped and nudged constantly. We had parked far away in the free parking, which meant at least a twenty-minute walk back — and of course, I had to pee.

"Can I use your restroom?" I asked a shop owner who hadn't finished locking up for the night.

"Restrooms are for paying customers," he replied, to my utter shock.

"I'm pregnant," I said. "I'll be quick."

"Paying customers," he repeated.

"Fine," I snapped. Vanity had heard the entire exchange and said nothing, which made it obvious she had no plans to go inside and buy anything to help.

By the time we finally reached the car, my bladder felt like it was about to explode.

"I have to pee so bad it hurts," I whined to Vanity, standing outside the car even after I heard the beep of the door unlocking. Maybe she'd forgotten how it feels to have a baby pressing on your bladder. Or maybe she just didn't care. She'd dragged me around all day running errands and hanging out with friends, refusing to let me out of her sight. But I wasn't getting in the car without using the bathroom. Peeing where I stood wasn't out of the question at this point.

"Well, come on, get in."

"I need to pee."

"We'll stop at a gas station."

Peeing on the ground in what I was wearing would've meant taking off my sweatpants completely if I didn't want them soaked — and I didn't — so I got into the back seat. Sitting down made the pressure even worse.

"Hurry," I whined again.

Hyper-focused on not peeing myself, I didn't even notice that Vanity had gotten on the freeway instead of heading toward a gas station.

"How far is a bathroom?"

"We'll be home in ten minutes," she said.

"I thought you were going to a gas station. I'm going to pee in your back seat," I threatened.

"I know you're old enough to hold your bladder."

I hated her in that moment. I didn't even bother responding. Instead, I broke the time up in my head. You can get through anything one minute at a time. I just had to hold it for five minutes — twice. I looked out the window and pretended we were racing the cars we passed, and losing against the cars that passed us. It felt like we were losing more than winning. I checked the clock to see how much time had gone by. Looking up at the freeway signs, I saw my street was just four miles away. I watched each exit tick by until she finally got off the freeway.

I got out of the car, walked straight to the bathroom, and then went to bed without saying a word.

***

In the morning, I woke up to find Vanity gone. I was so tired and worn out from yesterday's events, I was sure she had taken the opportunity of me being fast asleep to go visit one of her guy friends and decided to stay the night.

Getting out of bed, I immediately had to use the bathroom. After I peed, I still felt immense pressure, and my back spasmed as I walked to the kitchen. I poured myself a large glass of orange juice, drank half of it, set the cup on the cluttered dining room table, and plopped down on the living room sofa to turn on the TV.

I was watching another episode of birthing stories when I started having cramps—similar to period pains, except instead of the usual sensation of a knife slicing sharply across my lower belly, it was happening around my hips and lower back. I propped a pillow behind me and tried to relax through another episode.

Eventually, I got up from the floor and went to the dining area to grab the cordless phone.

"Hello?" I said when I heard it pick up.

"Yes, Nicole," Vanity answered impatiently.

"I think I'm going into labor."

"You sound way too calm to be going into labor."

"I'm having contractions."

"It's probably Braxton Hicks. Drink a full glass of water, wait 30 minutes, and see if it helps."

"When will you be back?"

"Girl, I'm out. Drink some water. Actually, hop into the shower and let the warm water hit your belly. I'll be back soon."

I heard the dial tone click, letting me know Vanity had hung up, so I placed the phone back on the receiver and headed toward the hall closet to grab a towel and washcloth.

Vanity's shower wasn't too different from the hall bathroom except that it was a walk-in and didn't have a tub, which I preferred. But since she was gone anyway, I made my way through her cluttered bedroom to the master bath and turned on the shower. It didn't take long for the water to reach the right temperature, and I stepped in.

The steam made the bathroom feel like a sauna, and the warm water eased my tension. I suddenly felt sleepy. I guess after having five kids, Vanity did know a thing or two—because I was relaxed, and the cramping had faded. Not sure when she'd return, I crawled into her bed, which was far more comfortable than my twin, and fell asleep.

I woke up to the sound of Vanity clunking around her room, setting her purse and Motorola down on the nightstand. Reaching for the remote, she turned on the TV and clicked through the guide until she landed on a Lifetime movie that was just starting.

I started to sit up. The films on the Lifetime Movie Network always gave me anxiety—the women were either being cheated on, stalked, abused, battered, or worse.

"I think I'm just going to go to bed," I said, climbing down from the bed a few minutes into the movie. Vanity was glued to the screen and just gave me a nod, not taking her eyes off the TV.

I barely made it past the television when a sudden gush of liquid splattered down my legs and onto the floor.

"Oh my God," I said, staring at the mess in shock. "I think I just peed myself."

"Your water just broke," Vanity replied calmly.

I barely registered her response before a surge of pain tore through my stomach, back, and legs. Doubled over, I let out a scream.

"Now," Vanity said, grabbing her purse. "Now, you're in labor."

Her Baby Is Born

Vanity came to an abrupt halt in front of the emergency entrance, and I couldn't have been more relieved to finally make it.

Contractions continued to rip through me, and I could hardly stand straight. Continuing to take steps with contractions coming less than a minute apart was proving impossible.

Just inside the lobby entrance, I stopped and began to squat.

"She needs a wheelchair," the front desk clerk told another woman.

A transportation nurse came racing down the hall with a wheelchair.

"Oh no, honey, let's get you to labor and delivery."

Another nurse speed-walked to join the one pushing me.

"How far along is she?"

"Thirty-eight weeks," Vanity answered.

"Who is the doctor?"

"Doctor Booth," Vanity stated.

Checking the tablet the woman held in her hand—I assumed to look at the schedule—she said,

"I don't think we have time to wait for her. I'll page the doctor on call. This baby is coming now."

The contractions started to become too much to bear sitting down, and I got out of the wheelchair, shocking the nurse who was pushing me. I dropped back into a squatting stance to push.

"You need to sit down, honey," she said, grabbing me around the waist to guide me back into the wheelchair.

I sat uncomfortably back down, and she began to wheel me forward. When another contraction came, I gripped the arms of the wheelchair as we entered the elevator.

Finally, we reached the delivery room, and I was instantly back out of the chair. My body demanded I stand up.

"Honey, we don't want you to have your baby on the floor," she said, leading me to the bed.

Lying down on the bed was uncomfortable, and I started to sit up.

"I can't lay down," I screamed at no one in particular as I attempted to stand again.

"Oh, wait. Don't go anywhere!" a nurse who seemed to have appeared out of nowhere said as she took my arm and wrapped a blood pressure cuff around it.

Another nurse took my other arm and inserted an IV line.

"Okay, hon, I'm going to check your cervix. You're going to feel some pressure."

I took a deep breath. It couldn't be worse than the pressure I was already feeling, so I nodded at her.

"Go ahead and call the doctor in. She's ready to start pushing."

Not even a minute later, the doctor walked in with a smile.

"Looks like we're about to have a baby today," he said. "Are we doing an episiotomy?" He looked at Vanity.

I didn't want an episiotomy. I had watched hours upon hours of birthing stories during my pregnancy—I knew it wasn't always necessary. The doctor had no way of knowing if a woman would tear and that a surgical cut was needed to prevent it. And even if it did occur, it was better for it to happen naturally. But before I could object, Vanity told the doctor yes.

I let out a scream—not from the pain of the cut, but from the anger that the cut was made without the doctor consulting me, his patient. I guessed you had to be an adult to receive that basic courtesy. I screamed because even my labor wasn't my own.

I was just a teen, and apparently not worth consulting.

"When you feel the next contraction, I want you to really push," the nurse assisting the doctor said. "Really give it your all this time."

Three pushes later, I heard a baby crying—and Vanity making a phone call.

"She had the baby… Yeah… A beautiful boy. Head full of hair too… haha… Yeah… You and your sisters were practically bald when you were born."

The nurses were busy attending to the new soul I had just brought into the world—getting his weight, measuring how long he was, giving him his first bath, washing all the vernix out of his luscious jet-black curls, and dressing him in the smallest, cutest outfit and beanie I had ever seen.

"Are you planning on nursing or bottle-feeding?" the nurse asked me.

"Hmm," I said, unsure how I should respond, knowing my son was going to be adopted. Once again, I had never asked any questions about what would happen after the birth—or how I was actually supposed to be in my son's life.

"She'll be nursing. Much healthier for the child," Vanity said, hanging up on whoever she had been speaking with—probably her daughter.

"Sounds good," the nurse replied with a smile. "I'll page a lactation coach to come in and speak with you."

Another nurse walked into the room, cheerful as ever. "I'm just going to take him to get his shot and bring him right back, okay?"

"Okay," I said.

With all the nursing staff finally out of the room, it went quiet. I started to drift off.

I was woken up by a nurse returning my son, followed by a lactation consultant ready to teach me how to properly nurse.

"It's important the baby has a good latch to make sure he's getting enough milk and gaining weight," she explained, placing my son in my arms.

When she finished, she left me to nurse him on my own. I must've dozed off again, because the next time I opened my eyes, a woman I didn't recognize was in the room. Vanity was gone. Vivian stood nearby with a car seat and diaper bag at her feet, holding my baby.

She must have taken him out of my arms while I slept—and knowing that made my stomach hurt, the way it always did when I started to feel anxious.

Given the circumstances, I didn't know why her holding my baby was making me feel this way. She was adopting him.

"Hi, Nicole. I'm Susan with Vital Records," the woman said. "I just need to get some information from you for the birth certificate."

"Alright," I said, sitting up to look at the form.

"Is your name and address correct?"

"Yep."

"Great. And what are we naming the baby?"

That question caught Vivian's attention. She walked to my bedside and pointed at the form.

"Jayshawn. Middle name King. Last name Alexander."

The woman wrote it down without even glancing at me for confirmation. I didn't have a name in mind anyway. I hadn't bothered to think of one. What would have been the point? I had known for most of my pregnancy that he wasn't really mine. I was the unpaid surrogate. The girl with no say.

"Thanks, hun," the woman said, looking up from her paperwork. "I got everything I need. You'll get a copy sent to the address on file."

***

"Congratulations! I heard your labor went well," said a nurse I hadn't seen before. "I have your discharge paperwork."

She handed me a packet and a goodie bag filled with sample-sized baby products and coupons.

"Thanks," I said, reaching for them.

"If you notice your son's eyes turning yellow, bring him back immediately. He may have jaundice."

"Okay."

"I'll have a wheelchair sent up to take you downstairs."

"Thanks."

As she made her way toward the door, she paused—like she'd just noticed Vivian and my baby for the first time.

"Aww, is this the little guy?"

"Yeah."

"So stinking adorable. And look at that full head of curly hair," she said, beaming. "That's a brilliantly nice head of hair!"

"Thanks. That's what everyone keeps saying," I replied, giving her a weak smile.

"I hope it doesn't all fall out, like it does with most babies."

She left the room. I took the next few minutes to change out of the hospital gown, clean myself up, put on a fresh pair of clothes, and brush my teeth in the sink just outside the bathroom.

Mine for the Summer

The wheelchair ride down to the car felt a lot faster than it had when I arrived. Maybe it was because I was no longer in pain, and I was about to enter uncharted territory. Everything was happening so quickly.

When we reached the lobby's sliding glass doors, I saw James already pulled up out front, waiting. He got out of the car just before I reached the door and took Jayshawn—strapped into his car seat—off my lap and placed him into the middle seat. I waited for him to finish before getting into the back seat next to my son. James and Vivian both climbed into the front, and we started to drive off.

I wanted to ask where we were headed—if it was their house or Vanity's. We had never discussed it. I didn't ask, though. I figured I'd find out soon enough.

We arrived at Vivian and James's house, and I let out a breath I hadn't realized I'd been holding. Because the baby shower had been a barbecue at the park across the street, I'd never actually gone inside. The house was dimly lit like Vanity's, with all the curtains drawn to block out the Arizona sun. I hated homes like that. I preferred the curtains open and light pouring in.

It seemed larger than Vanity's house, though maybe that was just because it wasn't as cluttered. In fact, there was no clutter at all. The dining table was bare, the countertops only held a few appliances, and that was it. The living room felt like the darkest room in the house, and after James showed me where I'd be sleeping, I returned to the living room with my baby in hand. I hadn't let either of them hold Jayshawn yet; I hadn't put him down since we arrived. I sat on the couch with the TV off as he slept curled up on my chest.

"Do you need anything?" James asked as he stepped into the room.

"No, I'm fine," I said. I wasn't sure how he felt about me being there, and with Vivian already seeming standoffish, the last thing I wanted was to be a burden.

He plopped down on the other end of the couch, making the cushions sink under his weight, and reached for the remote. He turned it toward me and pointed.

"This button here," he said, gesturing toward the small red button at the top, "turns the TV on. This one next to it turns on the cable box. Then you can press 'guide' or just flip through the channels till you find something."

"Okay. Thanks."

Vivian walked into the living room and sat down next to me.

"Why don't you go shower and relax while Jayshawn is sleeping?" she suggested.

I didn't respond right away. I was relaxed. The living room was dim, and Jayshawn was resting peacefully. If anything, I was hungry—but I figured I'd wait until they offered food. I decided not to fight with her, not on the first day in her house.

"Where are the towels?" I asked.

"I put a towel and washcloth in the bathroom already. While we were at the hospital, my mom dropped off some of your things."

"Oh," I said, standing.

Maybe she didn't want me getting too attached, which I guessed was for the best. He was her son now. I was just the teenager who had given birth to him. I handed a still-sleeping Jayshawn to Vivian and headed for the shower.

***

Four weeks went by, more or less the same. I spent most of my time sitting on the couch, staying out of Vivian and James's way, holding my infant son.

James popped his head into the living room each morning to greet me and Jayshawn before heading to work. Vivian did the same shortly after.

Vanity had dropped off a breast pump so I could express milk, allowing Vivian and James to bottle-feed Jayshawn when they were home. Holding and feeding a baby was how parents bonded with their newborns, and they wanted to bond with him. I understood that. But pumping felt redundant. He could nurse directly from me. Instead, I had to hook myself up to a machine, collect the milk, pour it into a bottle, and then hand it over so they could feed him.

It had felt like an unnecessary amount of work, especially because after he finished the bottle, the machine needed to be cleaned for the next use.

I could tell Vivian sensed my annoyance with the situation, but I really couldn't help myself. She wasn't the one being hooked up to a loud machine for forty minutes at a time—twenty minutes on each side.

James had been happy to hold and feed Jayshawn, and as much as I had wanted to be the one holding my son, it was nice to see how happy he looked with him. Maybe Jayshawn would receive plenty of love and be okay with Vivian and James after all. My son would have a father—something he wouldn't have with me—and a mother.

Being able to remain in my son's life and ensure he was being raised in a way I approved of mattered to me. Still, it was hard playing the role of nothing more than a wet nurse while being his mother. I fought the urge to object every time I had to hand him over. Fought the urge to say I didn't want to pump anymore because it hurt and felt like a waste of time.

"My mother tells me school is starting up next week," Vivian said, standing near the kitchen counter while I washed out used bottles.

I had known I'd be made to go back to school, but it had been in the very back of my mind. Despite knowing it was coming, it was the last place I wanted to be. By the time school let out for the summer, I hadn't had friends anymore.

I had only ever really made two: Destiny and Laquanna. I met both girls on the first day of school. Destiny, I met in my fourth-period class—the one right before lunch—and at lunch, I was introduced to Laquanna. I had been desperate to make a friend and determined not to eat alone in the bathroom like I had done in middle school and elementary. That whole first day, I barely paid attention to class. I spent most of the time going back and forth in my mind about who I should speak to and who might make a good friend.

By fourth period, I forced myself to just speak up—and that's how I met Destiny, who introduced me to her best friend. Even though I met Destiny first, I ended up becoming closer with Laquanna since she lived just a block over from me in the same neighborhood.

Once it got around school that I was pregnant, Destiny told me her father didn't want her hanging around me anymore because I was a bad influence. Laquanna stuck it out for a bit longer, but ultimately, she was too embarrassed to be seen with me. A full-fledged pregnant teen.

So, with a foster sister who wanted absolutely nothing to do with me on campus—or at all—and no friends, and a baby who needed me, school just didn't seem important.

"I would like you to continue to pump, though," she added, and I brought my attention back to the conversation, nodding without looking up, my hands still submerged in soapy water.

So this was it.

I had served my purpose.

I had the baby.

I handed over the baby.

And I was providing milk.

There wasn't much more they needed from me. I had served my purpose.

I already knew I was on borrowed time. I couldn't live with them forever. I still technically lived with Vanity. I knew I'd have to go back to school once it started. I had agreed to let Vivian and James adopt my child. So why did my chest suddenly feel tight? Why did the mere mention of school and having to leave their home upset me so much?

I finished rinsing out the last bottle and returned to the living room. Jayshawn was sleeping peacefully in his baby swing. I picked him up, waking him gently. He looked at me with his large brown, almond-shaped eyes. I cradled him in my arm and ran my palm lightly over the soft pile of curls on top of his tiny head.

Holding him helped to calm the anxiety of my impending departure.

***

It was early in the morning when Vanity came to her daughter's house to collect me. She wore a form-fitting dress, a jean jacket, and heels—probably coming straight from the casino to Vivian's house.

I had all my things packed and waiting by the door. I was glad Jayshawn was asleep when I left. He would wake up, and I knew Vivian would feed him with a bottle of breast milk from the freezer, thawing out the oldest one first. I had made sure to label each bag with dates to make feeding easier. She probably had a little less than a week's supply, which meant I'd need to come back in a few days to drop off more.

Knowing that—knowing I'd be back—was the only reason I didn't break down and cause an upsetting scene.

I would be back.

Most likely Friday evening.

I could get through five days.

Postpartum

This morning, while getting dressed for school, I had made sure to roll up a wad of toilet paper so my engorged breasts—leaking milk—wouldn't show through my T-shirt.

I was in second period when I felt the stabbing pain of my milk coming in. My body was telling me it was time for my child to have another feeding. Babies ate every two to three hours, the nurse had explained to me when my son was less than an hour old. She had taught me how to properly latch him onto my breast to ensure he got a good flow of milk. My body was doing what it was supposed to do for the survival of my child and hadn't quite gotten the memo to stop the supply.

I started to feel the wetness against my breast and knew the thin toilet paper I'd wadded up wasn't enough to prevent the leakage from showing up as two large circles around my nipples. I crossed my arms tightly over my chest and leaned my head down onto the textbook I hadn't even opened. I said a silent prayer, hoping the teacher wouldn't think I was sleeping and call on me to check.

Because I didn't think it was possible for me to feel any more embarrassed.

I had grabbed a seat along the wall near the back of the classroom—not too far from the door. I'd been doing that all week in every sit-down class, and I had skipped dance altogether. Coming to school was a nightmare, and being away from my son was physically painful.

I tried not to grimace too much, but I had left Vanity's house this morning without remembering to take pain medication.

Letting out a sigh—because that was all I could do to keep from crying—I uncrossed my arms and sat up. My armpits were too tender to touch, and I couldn't sit like that any longer. So I sat up straight, accepting that there wasn't much more I could do but hope no one noticed me. Hope I had made myself invisible just by sitting in the back and keeping my hand down.

Raising my hand to participate in class discussions—or speaking to anyone, really—was out of the question. I wanted to be invisible. Just a quiet girl in the back of the room, left alone.

Finally, the two loud chimes rang over the speaker, signaling the end of class. Students started rushing toward the door, and I leaned down to grab my nearly empty backpack and do the same.

"Nicole, can you come see me?" my history teacher called out before I could make it out.

I froze. I guess he had noticed me. Noticed that I hadn't opened my textbook once or taken a single note all week.

Students continued to pour out of the room as I slowly made my way to the far-left corner where my teacher was now sitting behind his desk. He looked at me with kind eyes, but my guard stayed up. We were now alone in the classroom, and that made me nervous.

I glanced around, even though I already knew no one else was there.

Was he going to be weird about this?

I reached his desk and stood there, but instead of facing him directly, I turned slightly, angling myself toward the unused blackboard.

"I just want to check in with you—are you okay?"

Wait. He just wanted to check in. See if I was okay.

Someone who didn't want anything from me. Someone who wasn't trying to take advantage.

Okay. Wow.

This was new.

I wasn't okay—not even close—and him just asking that, just noticing me, made me realize that I didn't want to be invisible. I wanted—needed—someone to care enough to check in.

I had been trying to manage my emotions. The feelings of betrayal. From literally everyone.

I hadn't been able to reach Vivian all week. Vanity was too busy celebrating the fact that there was now a baby to care for—that the child was mine. That he had been taken from me and how hard that actually might be? That hadn't even crossed her mind. My caseworker hadn't called. My Court Appointed Special Advocate—the one who had found the "perfect" family for my son—hadn't reached out either. All the people who were supposed to be in my corner were scattered in different corners of the world.

And somehow, with just one simple question, all those feelings rushed to the surface.

I didn't want to cry in front of my teacher. School had only been in session for a week. Taking a deep breath, and steadying my voice, I said, "I'm fine."

Maybe if someone had checked in sooner, my answer might have been different.

"Okay. See you next week," he said.

I think we both knew it was a lie. But thankfully, he didn't push it. I was already feeling awkward and uncomfortable just being alone in a room with him. Without giving him another glance, I walked out of the classroom and headed straight for the nearest bathroom.

I turned on the faucet and loosened my halter top, letting the straps fall. Leaning over the sink as much as I could, my breasts felt like heavy rocks in my hands, so engorged it hurt to hold them. The slight pressure I applied to manually express the built-up milk was so painful I bit my lower lip just to keep from yelping.

The physical pain made it impossible to ignore the emotional pain I'd been trying to bury. Normally, I found strength in the strength of other people. But I was alone—in a high school girls' bathroom. There were no motivational posters on the walls. Just cracks, peeling paint, and scribbled insults from girls lashing out at other girls. In this moment, there was no one modeling courage like the women I watched on birthing shows. No peer who understood. No adult to help me navigate this postpartum body. My body had no resilience left. I could no longer hold back the tears.

I wanted to—but they poured out anyway, like a dam finally split wide open.

***

When I finally left the bathroom, I decided not to go to my next class. Instead, I ducked into the school library to hide out. The library had a computer station—two long rows with maybe fifteen computers on each side. There was a main desk for the librarian and a few scattered tables for students. All the books were on the far side of the room.

I sat at a table near the back, figuring the librarian wouldn't bother me if I looked like I was doing something. I took out a notebook and a textbook and started doodling. There were a couple of other students around. My eavesdropping told me they actually had assignments to do. They weren't ditching, like me.

I stayed there until I heard the lunch bell ring. I took my time walking to the cafeteria. I wasn't in a rush to see anyone. The two girls I'd been friends with last semester hadn't reached out all summer. And even though I wasn't pregnant anymore, it still felt weird to seek them out now.

So, I was back to eating alone.

No more hiding in the bathroom to eat, though. At least I'd grown past that.

I scanned the lunch lines—pizza, burgers, burritos—trying to decide which one was the shortest. Taste-wise, it was a gamble either way. The burger cheese might be melted or might still be cold. The pizza could be fresh or dried out under the heat lamp. The burrito might have too much meat and no beans, or just be a cheesy mess.

I decided pizza was the safest bet and the line seemed to be moving fast enough. I stood behind a group of girls chatting about their weekend plans, completely wrapped up in their own world.

When I made it to the front of the line, the lunch lady—who looked like she should've retired five years ago—greeted me without much expression.

"Cheese or pepperoni?"

"Pepperoni," I said, sliding my school ID across the scanner for my free lunch.

I took my tray and left the crowded lunchroom to find a spot under the palm tree in the courtyard. It was quiet there, shaded, and most importantly—isolated. I ate slowly, taking my time. When the bell rang, signaling the end of lunch, I didn't move right away.

I had no desire to go to my next class. But I couldn't stay in the courtyard either. Security guards patrolled campus to make sure students were either in class or on their way with a tardy note. If you were caught just wandering, they'd walk you to class—and if it happened often enough, they'd send you to the office. I didn't want that.

I hated my next class anyway. The instructor seemed to hate me. She didn't say anything outright, but the vibe was clear—like she took it personally that I didn't understand the material.

I walked through the building, past several classrooms, until I found the bathroom. I slipped into the handicap stall and sat on the cold floor.

Twenty minutes passed.

Eventually, I got up and went to the water fountain. That's when I noticed a boy who looked like he was wandering the halls too. He wasn't in any of my classes, which made me wonder which one he was ditching. He was tall and slender with sad, downcast eyes—the same worn-down look I'd seen on kids in the group home. Still, I doubted he was a group home kid. His clothes didn't seem ill-fitting, which was usually a dead giveaway—kids in the system mostly wore whatever hand-me-downs or donated items happened to be available in their size.

I figured he must've had his own issues at home. There had to be some reason, just like me, that he didn't feel like sitting in a classroom learning things that didn't apply to real life. Not when there were so many other things to worry about.

I reached the water fountain and took a slow sip, not in any kind of rush. When I lifted my head, I noticed he had sat down against the wall a few feet away, watching me.

"I've seen you around before," he said. "You're Nicole, right?"

If I hadn't been "the pregnant girl" last semester, I might've been surprised he knew my name—but it made sense. People remembered the pregnant girl.

"Yeah."

"What class are you ditching?" I asked.

Whatever mood he'd been in seemed to fade away, replaced with a smirk. "At this point? All of them."

I sat down beside him against the wall. "Why are you hiding out in the halls?"

We sat and talked about a whole lot of nothing until the final bell rang, signaling the end of the school day. It was nice—just having someone to talk to. Life as a teen mom could be isolating. People thought once the baby was born, things would go back to normal, but they didn't. The friends who'd disappeared didn't come running back just because I wasn't pregnant anymore.

When the halls filled with students leaving class, I stood up and blended in with the crowd, disappearing into the noise like everyone else.

***

I took the city bus home from school. Most kids at my school did—public transportation was free if you swiped your student ID. If you didn't have it, the fare was sixty cents, which bought you a transfer good for three hours. I knew this because I lost my school ID often and had to either dig for loose change in Vanity's room or risk sneaking on the bus.

It wasn't that hard, honestly. After school, there were so many kids piling on at once that the drivers didn't have time to check every single fare. By the time I reached my stop, most of the bus had cleared out anyway.

As usual, Vanity wasn't home when I got back. I headed to the freezer to grab the milk I had pumped over the past couple of days—but it was gone.

This wasn't the first time. Vanity had apparently dropped it off with Vivian while I was at school. Which meant—again—I didn't get to see my son.

Furious, I picked up the receiver and dialed Vanity.

"You took the milk to Vivian?"

"Yes, I did."

"Why didn't you tell me—or wait until I could go?"

"I don't plan my errands around you, Nicole."

"Well, when will I get to see my son?"

"You need to calm down and remember—she adopted him. He's her child. She needs time to bond with him, and you need to give her space to do that."

"Well, you guys said I could see him. So when's the next time?"

"Depends on her schedule."

"She never answers when I call. I've been trying," I said, the frustration cracking through my voice even though I was trying to stay level.

I hung up and immediately called Vivian's landline—like I'd been doing for weeks—hoping maybe this time she'd pick up and talk to me.

But no one answered. Again.

Screw School

The following week, I skipped all my classes again, hiding out on campus in either the bathroom, the library, or the football field—which was massive.

With Vanity gone most of the time, she usually missed the school's calls about my absences. And even if they tried to leave a voicemail, they couldn't—because I unplugged the answering machine as soon as I got home. That was typically when the school called anyway. No voicemail, no message, no proof. It worked for a while.

The only reason I even bothered taking the bus to school at all was the slim hope I might catch Dante in the science building halls during what would've been my last period. He was the closest thing I had to a friend. My only companion.

Whatever his situation was, something must've changed. Monday and Tuesday, I lingered around hoping to see him—but he never showed. I figured maybe I just missed him, maybe I went to the bathroom and came out too late. But then Wednesday came. Then Thursday. By Friday, I had to admit he was gone. Maybe sick, maybe transferred, maybe just over it. I hated how much I'd started looking forward to seeing him. Now I had to shove him to the deepest corner of my mind, where I stored everything and everyone I needed to forget.

With Dante gone, there was no reason left to even pretend I was going to school.

Monday morning, I got dressed, left the house, and hopped on the city bus. I sat in the back and watched as people got on and off. The route took about three hours from one end of town to the other—perfect, since school was about six hours long.

When the bus finally pulled into the terminal at the mall, the driver announced, "Last stop." I grabbed a snack from my backpack and waited for the next bus heading back in the direction of my foster home.

I got home just before 5 p.m. and found Vanity sitting on the couch, a letter in her hand and a scowl on her face.

"You can't seem to stay out of trouble," she said, waving the letter like a flag of my failure. "Ditching classes now—for weeks, this says."

I knew she wasn't going to hit me. Her anger wasn't about me—not really. It was about how my behavior disrupted her day, how it made her look like she couldn't control the teenager in her care. Still, the confrontation triggered something deep in me. I felt sick—too sick to speak. I didn't know if she even expected a response, but my brain always shut down in these moments. Blackout mode. Silence.

"We have a meeting with the school counselor," she added. "And I have to notify your social worker."

I nodded—or maybe I didn't. I couldn't remember. I just walked into my room and collapsed onto the bed, still in my clothes.

Sleep didn't come. Instead, I had a full-blown imaginary argument with her in my head.

You don't have any idea what I'm going through, I wanted to scream. You're too self-absorbed and out of touch. You have no empathy. Have you ever even stopped to think about how hard this is for me? No. Because you don't care. No one does.

I grabbed a pillow and screamed into it. The words were safe in my mind. I'd never say them out loud.

***

Dressed in sweatpants, a white T-shirt, and flip-flops, I sat on the sofa nearest the door, waiting for Vanity to finish getting ready for the school meeting about my ditching. Vanity never wore anything simple. She always had to leave the house with a full face of makeup, form-fitting, color-coordinated clothes, and heels.

She didn't seem to notice I wasn't speaking to her during the ten-minute car ride to the high school. A gospel track played on the stereo while she focused on driving, completely unbothered by my silence.

When we arrived, Vanity parked in the visitor lot near the entrance. I followed behind her as she strutted past the security guard and through the double doors into the main office.

A young woman at the front desk greeted us. "How can I help you?"

"We have a meeting at 10 a.m. with the guidance counselor," Vanity replied.

I sat down in one of the lobby chairs and looked up at the clock across the wall. 10:05. Of course, we were late.

The woman smiled politely and picked up the phone. "Nicole has arrived," she said, before hanging up.

Before Vanity could sit down next to me, a heavy-set woman appeared at the far end of the room, holding a door open. "Come on back," she said, looking at both of us.

I got up and followed them down a hallway to a conference room, where my social worker was already seated.

"You've been missing a lot of classes," the guidance counselor said, looking down at my attendance sheet.

She paused, waiting for a response, but I gave her nothing.

"You're expected to attend school 90% of the time."

Still nothing from me. I just stared back at her, stone-faced.

Because, honestly—what is knowing there are three types of rocks on Earth really going to do for me? The only thing dissecting a chicken last year taught me is that I can't eat chicken on the bone anymore.

"I looked over your schedule," she continued, glancing down at another paper. "I've been made aware you were pregnant last year. I know that can be distracting." She gave a sympathetic smile. "If you're finding the coursework difficult to follow, we could move some classes around or get you a tutor."

Everyone looked at me, waiting again. I didn't know what was going on in any of my classes. She was right—I had been distracted last year. But that hadn't changed. I was still distracted this year.

Like, what? Just have a baby and then forget the entire thing happened? Pretend nothing's changed and go back to school like normal?

"Classes are fine," I muttered, giving the counselor a bored look.

It was only sort of a lie. I had no clue what any of my instructors were talking about—but I also didn't care to figure it out. I was over it. Over school. Over Vanity. She pretended to care, acted like she wanted me involved in my son's life. So much for being part of her family. Her loyalty was to her real daughter—the one she gave birth to. Not me. I got the message loud and clear. I was done with all the so-called help from adults in my life.

"To ensure you're attending each of your scheduled classes," the counselor said, pulling papers from a file, "you'll be required to fill out this form, marking the time you arrived, and have each of your teachers sign off at the end of class."

I must've tuned her out because I had to actually read the form in front of me to catch up on what she'd just said.

My social worker finally spoke for the first time since greeting me when I walked in. "The law might allow children to drop out of school at sixteen or after completing the tenth grade. However," she added, locking eyes with me, "your case plan requires you to attend school."

***

Vanity pulls up to the roundabout designated for student drop-offs, and I exit the back seat of her red Mazda, walking toward the entrance and blending in with the crowd of students gathered just outside the gate. I had filled my backpack with a couple bottles of water, two small bags of Cheetos, and a couple of granola bars so I'd have something to eat when I got hungry.

Maryvale High School is not in the best neighborhood, and the school district has acted accordingly with its security. When school is in session, the campus is locked down. Security guards are stationed at the front gate, and the two side gates our school has are too high to jump over—horizontal bars make them impossible to climb. Once you walk through those gates, you're stuck at school until the bell rings and the exits open back up.

So I can't actually enter the school gates if I plan on ditching.

And I do.

I watched from behind some random boy's shoulder as Vanity's red Mazda pulled out of the parking lot and turned the corner. Then I headed away from the school toward the bus stop. I was tired of waiting. Tired of hoping Vivian would return one of my calls. Tired of waiting for Vanity to stop being okay with her daughter ignoring me. Tired of waiting for them to make good on the promises they both told me to get me to agree to let her daughter adopt my son.

Enough.

I didn't know Vivian's address. I should have. I stayed there for nearly two months. But I never took the time to look at a piece of mail or ask. All I had were the cross streets and my memory, which was going to have to be good enough—because I was going to see my son today.

I hadn't worked out a full plan for how things would go, but I knew if Vivian acted difficult, I would let her know I had changed my mind. I knew there was a window of time where birth mothers could revoke their consent, and I hoped I was still within that time frame.

I ended up having to take two separate buses to get to Vivian's house. The buses didn't typically turn and only ran north-south or east-west. But I needed to go southeast to even be in the neighborhood of Vivian's home. I got off the second bus and walked in the direction I remembered. When I spotted the park where the baby shower had been held, I knew I'd figured it out.

Now, just a few yards from Vivian's house, I was a ball of nerves. I sat on top of a picnic table, staring at her car in the driveway. She was most likely home.

I had never shown up to someone's house unannounced—especially not someone I knew had been ignoring me. I sat there staring, trying to collect myself. Demanding things out loud was never something I was good at. I needed time to think through what I was going to say.

Fifteen minutes passed and I was still role-playing what I'd say if she opened the door.

Hi, I was in the area and hoping to spend some time with my son.

Maybe I shouldn't say my son. I don't want to upset her.

I've been trying to reach you for some time now, so I wanted to see if I could catch you while you were still home.

That sounds intrusive, but it's the truth. It's literally why I'm here—in the park and not at school.

"You can't sit here forever, Nicole," I say out loud to myself, getting up from the picnic table and crossing the rest of the large open field of grass separating me from Vivian's house.

A police car drives by slowly, and I try to think nothing of it. But the neighborhood is quiet. I'm the only person in the park. There aren't many cars on the road—probably because adults are at work and kids are in school. I quicken my pace, knowing full well I'm one of the kids supposed to be in school.

My foot barely leaves the grass and hits the sidewalk when the police car turns sharply and lets out a quick burst of the siren.

"Nicole?" the officer says, rolling down his window as the car parks alongside the curb, blocking my path to cross the street.

I try to fight through the shakiness I feel and start to walk behind the police car to cross the street toward Vivian's. Before I can step off the curb, I'm flanked— one officer behind me, the other in front.

"Stop, Nicole," the officer says.

"You've been reported as a runaway. You need to come with us while we contact your guardian."

"I'm not a runaway," I say. "Sure, I ditched school… but I was just trying to see my baby."

"That's the other issue, young lady," he says, reaching for my hand—one I immediately pull back.

Vivian steps through her front door with my son on her shoulder, walking to the end of her driveway.

"Her foster mother is my mom, and she shouldn't be anywhere near here," she says to the officers, completely unsolicited, which enrages me.

"When I saw her sitting in the park, I called my mother to let her know she had ditched again and was outside my house."

"That's my son she's holding. I just want to see him," I say.

"We'll get that sorted later. For now, you're coming with us."

"Where?" I ask, panic rising in my throat.

"A holding facility."

"…But why?" I start to struggle against the officer's grasp. He's far stronger than me, and before I know it, I'm placed in the back of the police car. I slide over to the right-side passenger seat, trying to get a better look at Vivian—trying to make out what she's saying—but I can't hear anything with the windows rolled up.

Detention

I watched Vivian as she walked back into her house while the officers pulled away with me still in the backseat. I was hot, and the sides of my wrists felt raw from the metal handcuffs rubbing against them.

"I'm really hot back here. I feel like I'm suffocating," I whined. Part of me knew better.

"The AC is on," the officer said.

I could hear it, but I didn't feel it at all—not with the plexiglass divider blocking the airflow.

"I can't feel it," I said again.

The officer in the passenger seat turned the AC higher, but all that seemed to do was make it louder. It still didn't cool off the back of the car.

I wrestled with the handcuffs, trying to shift them off the bony part of my wrist as we drove farther away from the neighborhoods and corner stores, leaving the city behind. Once we got on the freeway, maybe it was starting to cool down, but I still felt like I couldn't breathe. The more cars we passed, the more self-conscious I became sitting in the back of the police car. I could see straight into the passenger seats of the cars we passed, which meant they could see me too—clear as day. I wondered what they were thinking. My rational brain knew they didn't know me from Adam, but still, I was embarrassed. Embarrassed to be seen like this, to be mistaken for a criminal—a junkie, a thief, some misfit teen who was a burden to society.

Forty-five minutes later, we pulled up to an old brown brick facility surrounded by a massive gate, manned by security. In large block orange letters, the name Durango was printed above smaller lettering that read Juvenile Detention Center.

I couldn't make out how large the building was since we entered from the back, but it seemed to take up the entire block. There was no more road beyond it. Past the security gate, thick metal sliding doors waited. Staff had to be buzzed in. We passed through one set of doors, only to be stopped a few steps later by another set, which also required someone on the inside to buzz us through into the actual detention center I had somehow landed myself in.

Stepping through the doorway, I felt the despair hit me in the chest. Kind of like when you walk into a hospital and immediately smell death all around you. I took slow, deliberate breaths, trying to calm my nerves. It was just an old building. Just gray walls and metal. I wasn't entering a death chamber—I was just entering juvie.

"Alexa," I heard a woman nudge a short brunette, "how did your date with that online guy go?" she asked, grinning.

I glared at them, irritated. Could they not read the room? No one was happy here. Shut the fuck up with all that laughing and talking about your enjoyments. At least pretend to be miserable like the rest of us. I was still handcuffed, standing there like some kind of criminal, and they were going on about their damn date night?

I didn't know if they felt my stare burning into them or what, but they finally stopped talking and approached the officer.

"You can un-cuff her," one of them said, and the officer left without another word.

"Have a seat," she said to me, motioning toward a row of green plastic chairs lined along the back wall.

I followed the woman's directions and sat on the green plastic chair, rubbing my wrists, which were now tender and had deep grooves from where the tight handcuffs had pressed into them.

"Nicole Hayes," an elderly woman with thick glasses called my name. I looked around to see where the voice had come from and spotted an office door open that I hadn't noticed before. "Come with me. I'll get you processed in."

I followed her into a rectangular-shaped room where she had me stand against a wall to get my picture taken and confirm my name and date of birth. She printed the info onto a thin white wristband.

"This is your identification," she said. "You're not supposed to take it off."

With the plastic band now secured around my wrist and the intake process over, I was led down a long hallway to a room that resembled a locker room.

"You're going to step into the shower stall and disrobe," the old woman ordered, her tone dry and disinterested—like she'd said the same line a thousand times before. "Hand me your clothes when you're finished, and I'll have an outfit waiting for you."

I stepped into the stall—my head and legs exposed from either end—and took off my sneakers, sweats, and white T-shirt. A small gray button stuck out of the shower wall. I hesitated.

"You need to hurry it up. I have other things to do," the woman barked.

"Mmm. If you want to just pass me the clothes I need, I already showered today."

"Everyone who steps in here is required to shower. Do I need to call for support, or are you going to do as instructed?"

I pushed the button and immediately jumped back as ice-cold water sprayed from the nozzle. I pressed myself into the corner of the stall, trying to avoid as much of the water as possible, and waited for it to turn off on its own.

I grabbed the towel hanging on the door of the stall, wrapped it around myself, and stepped out to find a gray T-shirt, blue khaki pants, long white socks, and a pair of shoes that looked like blue knockoff Converse waiting for me on a bench. Realizing the woman wasn't going anywhere—and wasn't planning to look away—I dropped the towel and got dressed.

I had barely finished tying my second shoe when she was already heading toward the door, expecting me to follow. We didn't pass anyone in the halls, and I was thankful for that because the truth was—I was scared. I'd seen juvie in movies and on TV, and it was always brutal. I imagined I was being led to the lion's den. Only instead of a ground pit with a cage around it, I was surrounded by off-white cinder block walls and thick metal doors. An orange hue cast onto the floor—I couldn't tell if it was the lighting or the age of the floors. The air smelled like chemicals. Probably whatever cleaning solution they used to mop, even though at this point, the floor just needed to be replaced.

"Life is rarely like the movies," I whispered to myself, taking a deep breath and letting it out slowly before following the woman through the doorway and onto the unit. As wild as this day had been, I couldn't dwell. I needed to appear stoic and unbothered.

The unit was smaller than I expected. It wasn't a circular pod like in the movies, with screaming girls yelling "fresh meat" and threatening to beat me up. No one was even there—just a woman behind a desk. It was quiet. The woman who'd brought me there turned and left, and the one behind the desk stood and walked toward me.

"Nicole," she said, glancing at my plastic wristband. "My name is Mrs. Stone—or Officer Stone. I work the evening shift with my partner, Officer Morgan, who'll be here soon with the rest of the girls when classes end."

Class. They had class. Okay. Interesting.

I stared at her, waiting for whatever information she needed me to know. I tried to focus as she explained the rules and expectations, but my eyes kept scanning the room. This was going to be home for a while.

There were three shower stalls like the one I had to use during the intake process, and three sinks beside them. A rolling cart bookshelf stood near a wall shelf that held folded shirts—gray, blue, yellow, and red. A bucket sat beside it filled with underwear. So, we all shared the same underwear. Disgusting. There were also more pairs of blue pants in different sizes, and a bin of extra shoes— none of them looked new.

Nothing on the shelves looked new. The last shelf had fitted sheets and thin, terrycloth-like blankets folded up. Stacked against the wall between the shelves were mats that couldn't have been more than four inches thick, and they—like everything else in this building—were worn down and in desperate need of replacing.

"We operate on a point system," I heard her say as my mind started tuning back in. "Depending on how many points you gain or lose during the week, that determines your shirt level. Since you're new here, you start off as a grey shirt and have no privileges. After your first week—if we see you've learned the rules, or however long it takes you to follow directions—you can start to earn points. Red is the highest level and gets you the most privileges, below that is yellow, and then blue."

"What if I'm not here more than a week? I have a foster mom."

"You wouldn't have been brought here," she said, pausing for dramatic effect, "if you were going to be with us for less than a week."

She didn't wait for my reaction to that news. Instead, she handed me a fitted sheet and blanket and told me to grab a mat and follow her.

Knowing I'd be sleeping on one of those tattered mats, I tried to find one in decent condition. One whose foam still looked like it had some suspension left.

Walking down the long hallway made my mind flash back to scenes from The Green Mile, and I kept my head down while passing the doors on either side, not wanting to be a target of any onlookers. The halls were silent too. When the woman pulled out a large brown key to open the thick door to the cell, I realized no one else was inside. There wasn't even room for anyone else. The space was the size of a regular home's hallway bathroom.

I just stood there, unmoving, in the middle of the cell, coming to terms with my situation.

A metal slab stretched across one end of the far wall—the bed, I guessed— where the mat I was still holding was supposed to go. There was a metal toilet near the foot of the bed-slash-slab. Upon further inspection, I saw a sink built into the top of the toilet where a toilet lid should've been, with a drinking spigot. Gross. So I was going to be dehydrated my entire stay here, because there was no way I was drinking toilet bowl water. How was that even legal?

"Do you read?" the woman asked, pulling me out of my thoughts.

"Mmm, yes," I said, turning to look at her.

"You're allowed one book and a Bible in your cell. Come with me to pick one out."

I didn't think I'd be able to focus on reading anyway, but I had no idea how this place worked or how bored I might get in a cell alone. I followed her back out to the main area where I'd first seen the book cart. There weren't many books that caught my interest, and not wanting to take forever, I finally settled on a courtroom thriller. I knew I wouldn't be reading the Bible either, but I grabbed one anyway.

I stood next to the cart, unsure of what to do now that I had my two books.

"Go ahead and take a seat on the floor. The other girls will be returning from school shortly."

I did as I was instructed and sat down on the gray carpeted floor, leaning my back against the wall. My guard was up in anticipation of the girls' arrival. I knew from my time in group homes and children's shelters that these kinds of girls didn't respect weakness. They had a kick-you-while-you're-down mentality.

As I stared at the words on the page, I replayed the aftermath of my adoptive parents telling me and my sister we were moving to Florida "as a family." I wondered if they ever actually went to Florida—or if that was a lie too. Now that I was actually recalling the memory, I didn't remember seeing moving boxes. Wait… did anyone else even pack?

Damn. They really fooled me. And my sister too. We sat in the lobby of the Child Protective Services office, never once seeing our adoptive mother leave the building. I don't know what my child-mind thought was going on, watching people come and go until it was closing time. Maybe we thought our adoptive parents needed permission to leave the state.

What I do know is that at 5 p.m., a nice lady with a sympathetic look on her face came to collect me and my sister. That day, we were separated.

My sister was taken to one shelter that only had space for one more child, and I was taken to another that also only had space for one more.

I was terrified of my new surroundings. Newly abandoned and vulnerable without my sister—who I had never been separated from—I sat in the middle of a living room crying, feeling utterly lost and alone. A girl turned angrily from the TV and told me to shut up. I was eight. But that was the day I learned no one cared.

Those girls didn't have sympathy for me because all the girls sitting in the shelter had similar or worse things happen to them. They too had been discarded. No one saved them. No one came to their rescue. And if they survived—whatever horrible it was—they expected me to do the same. These girls who were due to arrive wouldn't be any different.

Crying, or doing anything other than putting on a tough face, would simply make me a target for bullying. So as much as I was feeling in this moment—as overwhelmed as I felt—I knew now wasn't the time to let my emotions get the best of me.

"Fix your face. Fix your face. Fix your face," I whispered to myself, breathing in and out slowly. "You got this."

The heavy door to the unit opened, and a short, stocky woman stepped in. Following behind her in a straight line were about twenty girls. They all had their hair pulled back in buns, shirts tucked into their blue pants, with white socks poking above knockoff Converse-style shoes without laces. Marching in uniform, they reminded me of the ROTC girls I used to see on campus. Not as crazy as I had let myself believe.

"It'll be okay," a girl in a grey shirt whispered in my ear after sitting down on the carpet next to me, clearly noticing how I'd eyed them all as they entered.

As the days passed, I learned that none of the girls on the unit were actually dangerous—just girls who'd found themselves in trouble after the system had let them down in one way or another.

The worst part of being in juvenile detention was simply being in the building at all. No natural light ever got in, forcing me to adjust to the constant orange hue the lights cast. The lights never turned off. The brick walls were dirty. It was always cold, and we only had thin blankets to sleep under. Showers were cold and limited to three minutes. Meals had to be speed-eaten within a small window of time, or else you'd be starving all night. And school—if you could call it that— was just a stack of fifth-grade worksheets and anger management videos.

Still, it took me a couple of weeks to adjust to the mundaneness of detention life and its rules. As remedial as school was, I started to look forward to it, because it was a chance to get out of my cell and off the unit. School also gave me the chance to talk to girls on my unit and the neighboring one that shared our hall. Outside of school or planned activities—which I could only participate in if I had enough points—we weren't supposed to talk to each other. The unit was meant to remain quiet and run smoothly.

Wake up. Complete hygiene. Walk to breakfast. Walk back for headcount. Go to school. Come back for headcount. Eat lunch. Count again. More classes. Back to the unit to read until dinner. Count again. Then either get sent to your cell for the rest of the night if you were a grey shirt, or stay out and watch a movie if you had privileges. Repeat.

I felt a little sad when girls got mail or were told they had a visit or phone call. I knew there was no one interested in writing to me or visiting me. Vivian had been ghosting me for months, and Vanity acted like it wasn't a problem that her daughter was a complete liar.

I despised everyone in my life.

They all claimed to care, to offer solutions—but the only problems they ever solved were their own. My problems be damned. Knowing this didn't make it hurt any less though.

The only thing keeping me from slipping into full-on depression was the fact that I was sixteen. In two years, I would be an adult, finally able to think and act freely on my own behalf.

I just needed to bide my time.

Release & Run

When the staff finally unlocked my cell in the early hours of the morning, I knew it was release day. Another placement. Another group home.

I gathered the belongings in my cell, dropping the sheets in the linen basket and the books I had borrowed onto the cart. I followed the guard back to the intake room where I had dressed out—and happily put back on the clothes I'd worn when I came in. Just like that, I was back through the basement exit, the same way I'd entered sixty days ago.

On the drive, I stayed quiet. I'd learned the routine by now. The staff would take me to the group home and maybe give me a lecture, a rundown of the rules, and what was expected of me.

Blah blah blah.

The girls were still at school when I arrived at the four-bedroom home. It looked really nice, actually. It didn't matter, though. What really mattered was how the staff treated the girls—and whether the girls were nice… or complete assholes.

After speaking with the staff, I learned my sister had aged out of the system and was now living in an apartment complex not far from the group home. I hadn't seen her much since we were separated at Promise House. I made up my mind—I was going to leave the group home at the first chance I got and go to my sister. She was eighteen now. She could adopt me or something.

It didn't take long to get my chance.

After dinner, everyone had chores, and the staff were both running around helping. I walked right out the front door in the midst of all the chaos. Slowly at first. But once I hit the sidewalk, I picked up the pace—hurrying up the street to get out of the neighborhood. I knew the buses well enough. I figured I'd be on a bus and long gone before they even realized I was missing.

The complex was run down—the kind of place with overgrown weeds and walls stained with graffiti. When I knocked on the door, it was Steven who answered. I sat down on the saggy couch, looking around at the stale living room. There was a TV on a wobbly stand, and the smell of cigarette smoke clung to everything.

"Hey, do you have any food or what?"

"All we have is noodles," he said with a shrug.

He made some in a pot while I sat on the sofa, staring at the TV, not actually watching.

"Where's my sister?" I asked.

Steven leaned back in his chair, a lazy smirk spreading across his face. "She's at her telemarketing job. She'll be back this afternoon," he said, swirling the amber liquid in his glass.

I sighed, not bothering to reply. After a few minutes of restless waiting, I went back to the couch and picked at some leftovers, my stomach tight with nerves. Steven, meanwhile, poured himself another drink. I didn't even try to count what number he was on—it was clearly too many.

He slumped into the chair across from me, his eyes glassy and unfocused. "You good over there?" he slurred.

I ignored him. I didn't want to appear too friendly. I knew his drunken type.

Then, out of nowhere, screaming ripped through the stale air. Loud, sharp, angry voices—girls yelling. I froze for a second, then shot up from the couch.

"What the hell is that?" I asked, looking toward the window.

Steven just shrugged and poured more whiskey into his glass. "Dunno. Probably some drama," he muttered.

I didn't wait for more. I bolted outside and found Rebecca—my sister— locked in a fight with another girl in the middle of the street. They had each other by the hair, yanking and clawing like wild animals.

"Rebecca!" I shouted, rushing toward her. "What are you doing?"

Neither of them even looked at me. The other girl threw a wild punch, missing Rebecca by inches. Rebecca retaliated by pulling harder on the girl's hair, her face twisted with rage.

"What the hell is going on here?" I yelled again, my voice drowned out by their screaming.

By then, Steven had stumbled out behind me, his shirt half-untucked, a drink still in his hand. He just stood there like an idiot, blinking at the scene in front of him.

"Well, this is awkward," he mumbled to no one in particular.

The small crowd of onlookers didn't help.

"Stop it, both of you!" I yelled, stepping closer—but the girls were too far gone.

Rebecca was snarling, "You think you can come at me, bitch? Over him?" She jabbed a finger toward Steven, who somehow had the audacity to look confused.

"Oh, please," the other girl snapped back, her voice dripping with venom. "He was with me first. You're just mad you're second choice."

"Second choice? He's my man, you desperate skank!" Rebecca screamed, jerking the girl's hair so hard she winced.

Neither of them seemed to notice—or care—that Steven stood there doing absolutely nothing to defend himself or stop the fight. Useless, as always.

Eventually, it must've dawned on them that the hair-pulling wasn't getting them anywhere. They let go at nearly the same time, both red-faced and sweaty. The insults flew faster now. Rebecca shouted, "Go back to whatever gutter you crawled out of!" while the other girl snapped, "At least I don't have to beg for a man's attention!"

The other girl's friend finally stepped in, grabbing her by the arm. "Come on, let's go. She's not worth it," she said, dragging her away.

Rebecca stood there, breathing heavily. Her hair was a mess, and fresh scratches covered her arms and neck. I approached her cautiously.

"Are you okay?" I asked.

She waved me off, rolling her eyes. "I'm fine. It's nothing. What are you even doing here?"

"Nothing?" I asked, ignoring her second question. "Rebecca, she scratched you to hell!" I pointed at the angry red streaks across her skin. "What was that even about?"

Rebecca's lip curled. "She was trying to take my man," she muttered, glaring at Steven.

"Your man?" I scoffed, glancing at him. "You're fighting over him? He's a drunk. Are you serious right now?"

"Mind your business, Nicole," she snapped.

After a moment of silence, I lowered my voice. "Look, Rebecca, I need to ask you something," I said. "Can I stay with you? Just for a little while. I left the group home, and I don't have anywhere else to go."

Her face hardened instantly. "Nicole, I can't. I'm on probation. If someone finds out you're here, it could mess things up for me."

"You really can't help me? Not even for a few days?" I tried to keep the desperation out of my voice.

"I told you—I can't." Her tone wasn't apologetic. Just dismissive. "Go back to the group home. Maybe they won't be upset."

It hit like a punch to the gut, even though I'd seen it coming. Rebecca had never been the kind of sister to look out for me. I should've known better than to expect her to start now.

"Fine," I said tightly. "Can I at least use your phone?"

She sighed and dug it out of her pocket. "Make it quick," she said, handing it over. "I'm almost out of minutes."

I took it without a word and dialed the only person I could think of—an old friend from Promise House. Her name was Shantea. She'd aged out of the system a while ago and had her own place now. I didn't know if she'd say yes, but I had to try.

"Hey, Shantea," I said when she answered. My voice cracked a little. "It's Nicole. I need a favor…"

***

Staying with Shantea wasn't ideal, but it was a place to land.

Her apartment off Camelback, near Central, wasn't terrible—but it wasn't exactly homey either. The bedroom was a mess, with clothes piled on the floor because there were no dressers. The living room had a couch and a TV—bare essentials. In the corner, her baby's bassinet sat next to a deflated blow-up mattress. The kitchen had just a few mismatched plates and cups.

Shantea didn't work. Most days, she stayed in smoking weed or napping, occasionally heading out to visit some older Rastafarian guy who was obsessed with her. Or maybe just obsessed with girls in general. He always gave her free weed, and she seemed happy enough with that arrangement.

He was decent in a pinch if I was really starving. Ex-con, harmless pervert— he'd answer the door in his boxers with Girls Gone Wild blaring from the living room TV. But he didn't care if I raided his fridge or cupboards, so I just learned to tune out the moaning from the TV and eat.

I spent my time figuring out how to make things work for myself.

That's when Charles came into the picture.

I had met Charles on Black Planet while still at Vanity's house, but I didn't meet him in person until I was officially a runaway. He was much older than me—out of high school, out of college even—but younger than Rasta. That's what I liked about him. He had money—enough to buy me food or give me a little cash when I needed it. He wasn't around all the time, but when I stayed at Shantea's, he'd stop by now and then, dropping off burgers or a few bills, sometimes even paying for a hotel room.

Eventually, me and Shantea had a falling out over clothes Charles had bought me that she helped herself to. When I asked for them back, it turned into this whole ordeal. She refused to return them and kicked me out. I paced around for a bit, upset, then used a payphone to tell Charles what happened. He was mad and told me to go get my stuff.

Head-on confrontation literally makes my stomach hurt, though, so I waited until she left the house. Then I picked up a brick, threw it through her side window, and climbed in. The glass shattered cleanly. No neighbors seemed to notice. I grabbed all my things and left. We didn't talk after that.

I mainly relied on Charles while I was on the run—for food, a place to stay—but when he wasn't available, I had Terrance.

I met Terrance on Black Planet too. At first, I thought of him as a boyfriend. He was my age, a high school kid from South Phoenix, and we clicked right away. But after a while, he told me he was gay.

"It's not a big deal," he said one afternoon, grinning nervously. "We're still cool, right?"

"Of course," I said, brushing it off. I liked him for the company, and he liked me because I made it easier to avoid questions from his mom. When I stayed at his house, she just assumed I was his girlfriend.

Things fell apart after I stayed at his best friend Essex's house. Essex had this uncle—or maybe cousin—who gave me the creeps. One night, I woke up to find him on top of me.

I froze, unable to scream or fight back. When he finally got off, I retreated to the back room and stayed there until morning.

When it was time to leave, I avoided eye contact as I passed him. He was sitting on the couch like nothing had happened, smoking a blunt while Suga Free blasted from the speakers. Essex was obsessed with that artist—he had all the albums.

I never told Terrance or Essex what happened. I didn't want to explain. Most people don't want to think of their family as abusers anyway. I just stopped going to their houses altogether.

After that, I started hanging out with other runaway kids. There were so many of us—homeless or on the run, just trying to survive. We gathered at the library, parks, or behind abandoned buildings. Sometimes, we'd crash in empty apartments being remodeled or scheduled to be torn down. It wasn't much, but it was something.

I wasn't technically homeless—I was still a ward of the state. I could go back. I just didn't want to anymore.

I still had Charles from time to time, but I didn't always have a phone, so I mostly saw him after being released from juvie and placed in a new group home or with another foster mom.

The group homes—and even some of the foster homes—had rules, but I just stopped following them. No one really noticed.

The staff weren't exactly sharp, or maybe they just didn't care. You only needed to be 18 or older and able to read and write to work there, and they were paid minimum wage. Maybe it was just plain incompetence.

Shit. They didn't even notice me sneaking off to meet Charles.

One rule was that we girls weren't supposed to use the phone unless the staff knew who we were calling and it was someone on our approved list.

I'd sneak the phone after another girl had just finished using it.

Sometimes Charles would even drop off money. Then all I had to do was sneak out through the backyard, slide along the side gate, and meet him in his car a few houses down. Sometimes I'd sit in his car for half an hour, completely unnoticed.

With eight girls and one night staff member, I guess it was impossible for them to keep track of everything going on behind the scenes—unless another girl told. But they never did. Most of the time, I shared whatever food Charles brought with my roommate or asked him to grab something extra. My way of buying their silence.

My other foster mother was no better than Vanity, who was always busy running errands and doing various things, despite not actually having a real job. She had a nice house in the middle of what felt like nowhere, and I was the only person living in it. No foster sisters, no brothers, no dog—nothing. Even her husband lived in Tucson, which I found odd.

She was pleasant enough, but I think she got it in her mind that she was going to fix my so-called promiscuous behavior by trying to convince me I was ugly. It started subtly. She put me in old-fashioned church clothes and played gospel music every chance she got.

I remember she even took me to get a haircut. A boy's cut—maybe an inch or so of hair, tapered neatly in the back.

I was in the hallway bathroom, standing in front of the mirror, dolling myself up, and she decided she had to stand outside the bathroom door and tell me I wasn't "all that." Told me to stop admiring myself.

What?

I was so shocked.

Like, honey, I know I'm cute. You can't convince me otherwise. People my entire life—from childhood on—had told me I was cute. I could pull off any hairstyle. Take your bitterness somewhere, okay? At this point, I was almost 18, and her old ass wasn't about to come close to lowering my self-esteem.

She had an alarm system, but I learned to bypass it by cracking the back sliding glass door just enough that when she set the alarm, it still registered as closed. I used to sneak Charles into my bedroom pretty frequently.

One day she actually caught us—but didn't know it. She suspected something, probably because we weren't quiet enough. She opened the door and looked in. She didn't sit or touch the bed. Charles was under the blanket, still on top of me, just lower down. She asked if I was okay, and I told her I must've been sleep talking. She walked away.

Lucky for him, Charles Hanson wasn't on Black Planet.

I honestly can't remember why I ran away from her house.

This was one of those "it wasn't her—it was me" moments. She had her issues, but she wasn't bad. Her home was safe and secluded. Aside from sneaking Charles in through the barely ajar sliding door, I didn't cause her much trouble.

I think I ran because I was alone in that house all the time, bored out of my mind. There wasn't enough connection for me to bond with her or feel safe enough to trust her. During the day, I just hung out watching BET music videos—106 & Park with AJ and Free. She made meals. I didn't have chores or responsibilities. I hadn't even been enrolled in school. Maybe it was summer or something.

So, I ran from her home too. I hitchhiked my way back down into Phoenix to reconnect with the crew of homeless kids I had met, like some modern-day Boxcar Children.

On the Run

After staying with some homeless kids at the park, I got wind of a party. I hopped on the bus and headed west—59th Ave and Northern—where the party was supposedly happening. It was behind a convenience store and not too far from a graveyard.

Spooky.

I climbed the two flights of stairs and found the apartment. People were hanging out both inside and on the stairwell. The place was completely empty—no furniture, no electricity—just music blaring from someone's speaker. I figured someone had broken into the unit. It was common. Homeless teens I knew did it all the time, especially since half the complex was empty and being remodeled.

I was always hungry. Being a runaway with no money meant I never knew where my next meal would come from. I overheard one of the guys at the party mention that he was heading up the street to grab food.

"Hey, can I come with you?" I asked.

"Sure. Just give me one minute," he said, heading back upstairs. A moment later, he came out with another guy and a girl. "Ready?" he asked me.

Before I could even stand, the girl was already yelling.

"Who is this bitch? What in the hell?"

I froze.

She was yelling at the guy I'd just spoken to, clearly pissed. Turns out, she was his girlfriend.

"You coming onto my man, bitch?"

"No," I said quietly. I had only wanted something to eat, but clearly, that wasn't happening now. Not with her here.

Not wanting to make things worse, I left. I walked away from the party, heading down the stairs and out of the complex. I took my time, aimlessly making my way toward the main street. I wasn't really waiting for the light to change—I didn't have a plan. I was just tired and hungry.

The light turned red, and an old brown boxy car rolled to a stop with music blasting. The passenger window rolled down, and I saw a young Black girl sitting alone in the backseat. A guy sat in the front passenger seat, but he didn't say anything, so I ignored him.

"Where you headed, lil' ma?" the driver asked. He was heavyset, mid-twenties maybe, with a baby face. He sounded friendly, that flirty tone older guys always used.

"To get food," I said.

"Oh yeah? Where at? We're headed to McDonald's."

I lit up a little at that. McDonald's sounded amazing right then. I was starving. But I didn't have any money. If I did, I'd already be there.

"Hop in," he said casually, voice still friendly.

I didn't move.

I had just almost gotten into a fight over someone trying to feed me. I wasn't about to repeat that.

I glanced at the girl in the backseat, trying to get a read on her. She looked chill, not threatened, not annoyed.

The driver must've sensed my hesitation.

"We cool people, right?" he said, gesturing toward the girl in the back.

The light was about to change. They seemed like they were having a good time, music bumping, laughing. I didn't want to miss a chance to eat just because I was indecisive.

"Okay. Cool. Thanks," I finally said, and got in.

At the McDonald's drive-thru, he took everyone's order. I asked for my go-to: cheeseburger and fries, no pickles, with a Sprite.

We pulled out of the lot, music still loud, weed smoke now filling the car. I didn't smoke, but I didn't complain either. I was eating. That's all that mattered.

Eventually, we pulled into an apartment complex. Everyone got out of the car.

I made the mistake of following him inside.

Or maybe... the mistake I made was getting in the car in the first place.

Once inside, it didn't take me long to figure out that this man was a pimp. He went by the name Sin, and the quiet guy in the passenger seat turned out to be another pimp he was friends with.

I sat silently on the couch, reminding myself that not all pimps were bad.

Maybe I didn't need to be scared, I told myself, even though my gut was screaming otherwise.

The girl from the car didn't seem bothered at all. She was smoking and drinking on the couch, casually explaining how things worked and referring to Sin as Daddy. I was barely listening—my mind was racing, trying to figure out what I needed to do to get out of this situation.

Yeah... welp. I had always heard of pimps. I'd even managed to avoid a few when I lived off 51st Ave and McDowell with Vanity. I knew they were dangerous. Violent. They had their spots and their look. I thought I could spot them: high-priced cars, flashy jewelry, fresh haircuts, designer outfits, shoes always on point. They dripped with money and usually looked fine as hell too.

Welp, turns out I had been dead wrong for lumping them all together.

Every chance I got, I tried to run from Sin. I had no interest in selling myself for him—or even sleeping with him. But he didn't make it easy to leave. And when I did manage to escape, he would either find me again, or I'd get picked up by Phoenix Police. The officers would ask questions, sometimes even encourage me to call Sin so they could track him. But all I knew was his street name, and he never picked up when I was calling from the station.

So I'd end up in detention, waiting for another placement, and the cycle would repeat.

***

I had just been released and placed in yet another group home. I stayed long enough to walk in, sit down, and eat. That was it. I didn't even meet the other girls—ran away before they got home from school.

At this point, running away wasn't even a decision. It was instinct.

But why did I keep running?

What was I running from? What was I running toward?

I didn't know anymore. I just knew I had no intention of listening to staff or social workers. I walked straight out the front door, didn't bother packing clothes or food.

A few blocks away, I rounded a corner out of the residential neighborhood and onto a main street. I spotted a bus stop and felt a moment of relief. It was a good one—with a bench and some shade.

I barely noticed the car until it pulled up, startling me.

It was Sin.

How the hell had he found me again? I had just run away. Just.

I didn't have time to think, let alone run. He was out of the car before I could react. He grabbed me and shoved me into the backseat.

I scrambled for the door handle.

The child lock was on.

The car was already moving. My heart raced. I had no idea where we were headed.

"Let me out of this car," I demanded.

Wack.

He backhanded me hard across the face.

He was talking now, yelling something, but I couldn't process it.

Wack.

Another hit—same spot, harder.

Hot, silent tears spilled down my face.

I wanted to get away, but I was trapped.

We pulled into an apartment complex.

"Get out the car," he demanded, holding the door open.

I didn't move.

Getting out would only make things worse.

"Get the fuck out of the car," he said again, this time more controlled—like he was trying not to explode.

He reached for me. I scooted away, kicking at him.

He lunged into the backseat. His hands wrapped around my waist. I thrashed and kicked, desperate to break free, but a teenage girl fighting a grown man was no match.

He dragged me up the stairs as I struggled, crying, trying to make it hard for him to carry me.

"What's going on?" a man's voice called out.

I looked up.

There was someone standing in the doorway of his apartment just above us.

"Let her go!" the neighbor yelled.

Relief rushed through me.

Finally—someone was going to stop him from taking me.

It was short-lived.

Sin didn't obey the man.

"Mind your fucking business," he told the neighbor—and that was all it took. The man went back into his apartment and closed the door.

Still gripping me tightly, Sin managed to reach into his pocket and pull out a key. He used it to open the door to the apartment—the one right next to the man who had just turned away and shut me out.

The beating started the second that door closed.

The more I tried to escape him, the more vicious his strikes became.

I made a run for it, scrambling to the bathroom and spinning around to slam the door shut—but it didn't close fast enough. He was right behind me.

I was trapped.

Desperate, I climbed into the tub-shower combo and curled into the farthest corner, cowering against the tile wall.

Everything went silent after that.

When I came to, I was still on the shower floor.

I picked myself up slowly, everything aching, and slipped out of the apartment as quickly as I could.

I limped down the stairs and out of the complex, paranoid that Sin would pull up on me again—just like before—and snatch me back.

I kept looking over my shoulder, checking every car that passed.

I needed to get to a bus stop. I needed to get out of this neighborhood.

I found one and lingered, stepping off the curb every so often to see if the bus was coming.

No bus.

So I kept walking.

That's when I heard the short, sharp chirp of sirens.

A police car pulled up beside me and parked.

Just great.

He was going to run my name, see that I was in the system as a runaway, and haul me back in.

Welp.

At least I wouldn't have to worry about Sin for a while.

No More Chances

I was lying down on the shabby blue mattress with my knock-off Converse under my head for a pillow, reading my book, just waiting to be let out for dinner when my cell door clicked open.

"Hayes!"

"Yes," I said, happy for the interruption.

"You have a visitor," she said, making me sit up immediately.

"Really?" I asked, slipping on my shoes and tucking in my shirt like we were required to.

"Really. Let's go."

I followed the woman out of the unit, walking a few paces behind her with my hands behind my back.

We were headed to a conference room that felt like it was on the complete opposite end of the detention center based on how many turns we took to get there. A woman in a black skirt suit was already waiting when I walked in.

"Hi Nicole, nice to meet you," she said, holding out her hand.

"Ya," I muttered, barely placing my hand in hers out of politeness. I hate handshakes. Why can't "hello" just be enough?

"You're being held on a status offense," she began, leaning back in her chair with her legs crossed—getting straight to the point. "You have a court appearance coming up in the next couple of weeks to determine whether or not you'll continue to pose a flight risk. Social services and your case manager are also concerned about your irregular school attendance if you're released into a group home or foster care setting again. You know the State's main goal is to ensure your safety and give you as close to a normal upbringing as possible."

I nodded to show I was listening, even though the odds of me not running were slim, and I had zero intention of attending school. I decided against telling her any of that, though.

"I just want to let you know that, as of now, your caseworker wants to place you in a treatment center for troubled youth."

"Of course she does," I muttered, shifting in the office chair, trying not to fidget too much.

I was sitting too close to the attorney for her not to hear that. She smiled like she didn't take offense and reached into her laptop bag.

"I've actually heard really good things about the place," she said, pulling out a flier and sliding it over to me. "It's located in the mountains and is truly breathtakingly beautiful."

I took the flier and looked at the images—horses, lush green mountains with cacti scattered around, smiling staff and teens.

Mingus Mountain Youth Treatment Center

A Joint Commission-accredited behavioral health inpatient residential treatment center for girls. Our ability to treat and motivate our clients toward a positive, healthy future results in long-term success for our clients and their families. Our treatment program combines relational engagement, caring and well-trained staff, careful medical treatment, individualized psychotherapy and education, and numerous activities, including our unique equestrian program.

"I hear the property sits on 120 acres of land, and the girls enjoy their time riding horses and hiking," she added enthusiastically.

I didn't like her excitement. It made me want to tell her maybe she should go to Mingus if it was so great. The fact that she was selling it so hard made it obvious this wasn't a discussion—it was a done deal. They'd already decided where I was going.

And clearly, it wasn't going to be anywhere near Vivian or Vanity.

Not that I had bothered contacting Vanity after I ran away—I knew she'd alert the authorities and I'd end up back here anyway—but that didn't mean I didn't want to know where Vivian was. Or where my son was.

"How long will I have to stay there? I've already been here forever, and I haven't seen my son."

"Your son is being safely cared for. Right now, our main concern is your safety."

"I was told I would be able to be active in his life. That's not happening," I said, trying to keep the frustration out of my tone. "This place is too far. Why can't I go back to Vanity?"

"Given your incorrigibility and disruptive behaviors, Vanity's home is no longer suitable for your case plan."

"Well… can you at least get in touch with Vivian for me? Maybe schedule a visit?"

"I can certainly try. Do you have her number?"
Did I know her number?

I tried to think back to the wireless telephone and the pattern my fingers made when dialing Vivian's number. I repeated it in my head, visualizing the motion, and slowly recited it aloud. I gave her Vanity's number too, just in case. I watched as she wrote them down on her notepad, silently hoping she wouldn't forget to actually call.

"I haven't seen my son since he was probably two months old," I said again, trying not to sound combative or disagreeable as anger and sadness stormed through my mind like a brewing monsoon.

"We'll see what is said at court," she replied. "You'll have a chance to speak. Maybe you can convince social services that you're not a flight risk or a danger to yourself. But honestly… I think Mingus is a great placement for you."

Of course she did.

There was nothing else left to say. She excused herself, motioning to the staff member at the door to let them know we were done.

***

I was still thinking about what I could possibly say in court when my door clicked open.

Ever since the meeting with my attorney two weeks ago, all I had been able to think about was how to avoid getting sent up north to Mingus Mountain. I quickly folded the blanket on top of my mat and grabbed the shoes I'd been using as a makeshift pillow. I slid them on, my stomach tightening.

"You won't have time for a shower this morning," a staff member said as she entered. "The transportation vehicle is going to be here for you soon, if it isn't already. Brush your teeth and grab a breakfast tray off the cart."

I nodded and did as I was told, my body moving on autopilot. A heavy lump formed in my throat, and I fought back the urge to throw up. My fate would be decided today, and I still hadn't worked out how to convince the judge—or anyone, really—that I shouldn't be sent away.

I nibbled at the soggy pancakes in the Styrofoam container, the smell of syrup making my nausea worse, as I waited for the transportation officer to come take me to court.

I sat on the left side of the courtroom next to my Guardian Ad Litem. My caseworker and another woman representing the State sat at a table on the right.

The woman from the State spoke first.

"Since the beginning of the school year—August 8—Nicole has not attended any classes at any school."

The judge nodded. "Given your history of trouble and your current situation, I'm ruling that a locked-down behavioral health facility would benefit you greatly."

My history? The situation? I didn't have a history. I got pregnant. One pregnancy. That was it. Who would want to keep going to high school after that?

"Your son," the judge continued, flipping through a file that I assumed was mine. "The report I have here says he was adopted by a family of your choosing." He looked over at the woman from the State for confirmation.

"Yes," she replied smoothly. "Nicole's foster mother—her former foster mother—her daughter Vivian and Vivian's husband James were in the process of adopting the child when we were finalizing Nicole's family plan."

She paused, glancing at me briefly before continuing. "This is what both Vanity and Nicole advised the State at the time. So we withdrew our involvement and allowed all parties to handle the adoption privately."

"I agreed to an open adoption," I cut in. "I was handcuffed and brought to this detention center while trying to visit my son at Vivian's house."

"As far as the State is concerned," the woman responded coolly, "we have no knowledge of the terms of your private agreement with the adoptive parents. Any visitation would need to be discussed directly with them or possibly the agency they went through."

"I don't even know what agency they used," I said, feeling the heat rise in my chest.

"When this matter is resolved," she said, almost like she was placating a child, "your caseworker can look into that. Right now, we're here to address your repeated instances of running away and continued truancy."

"Being that you're in the State's care, we need to know your whereabouts. And the behavior you've been displaying makes that impossible. The State can't do its job—providing you with a healthy and safe environment—if we don't know where you are until you reach adulthood."

"You've made your point, Miss Blanche, and I agree," the judge said, barely glancing up. "Do you have anything more to say, Ms. Nicole?" He looked at me, clearly impatient, like he was already moving on in his mind.

"No," I replied, my voice tight with anger. I didn't even bother to look up and meet his eyes. Why did they even drag me here? Just to play pretend, like I had a voice or say in what happened to me? They'd already decided. The transportation officer had already been scheduled. The transfer already approved.

No one cared about my son anymore, or getting us back together. That was obvious.

"Court is adjourned," the judge said, standing and disappearing behind his bench like this was just another routine hearing. For him, maybe it was.

My Guardian Ad Litem followed me out of the courtroom and started in on some cliché, inspirational pep talk—but I wasn't listening. I couldn't listen. All the adults in my life were liars. Every last one.

I had trusted Vivian and Vanity when they promised me they were the perfect family to adopt my child. That I'd still be in his life because I was family too.

So much for family.

***

Oddly enough, even though I knew I was being sent up north to Mingus Mountain, I was happy to be leaving the detention center. When my cell door popped open, I was already standing, ready.

"Grab all your belongings and follow me."

I didn't have any belongings to collect, so I followed her immediately out of the cell and down the hall into the main pod area. None of the other girls had been let out for the morning hygiene routine yet, so I figured it had to still be early.

"Goodbye," I said out loud to no one in particular, stepping through the heavy metal doors to follow the staff member into the intake room—which also doubled as the discharge room.

I scanned the cubbies until I spotted a plastic bag with my name on it. Inside were the clothes I had on when I was arrested. I tore the bag open and pulled out my old sweatpants and a white T-shirt, then walked to the nearest stall to change.

"What do I do with these?" I asked, holding up the detention center uniform.

"Throw it in the basket against the wall and follow me," she said.

We exited through the basement—the same way I had entered every single time I'd been brought in. A thin woman, probably in her forties, was waiting outside next to a big white sixteen-passenger van to take me up north.

She opened the van door without saying much. I climbed in and slid into one of the middle seats. The van door shut with a loud click behind me.

Mingus Mountain

I had hoped my driver would need to get gas or that she was hungry herself so I could grab a snack—something that actually tasted like normal food—but she drove the entire two hours without stopping once.

We turned onto the 120-acre property from an inconspicuous dirt road just off the side of the freeway—one you'd completely miss unless you already knew it was there. I watched out the window as the van climbed the rocky dirt path toward the top of the mountain, passing cacti and tumbleweeds that lined the perimeter of the road.

I climbed out of the van, happy to finally stretch my legs and take in the desert scenery. After sitting inside a windowless building with no access to the outdoors for months, the hot northern sun actually felt kind of nice. Two dogs—both mutts—came running toward me, and I instinctively turned sideways, bracing for them to jump.

Just behind the dogs was my welcome committee.

A tall, thin man and an equally thin woman were approaching, followed by four girls.

"You must be Nicole," the man said. "My name is Dave, and I'm the Director of this year's treatment center." He did a half-spin, gesturing toward the mountain like I couldn't already tell where we were. "This beautiful woman here is Emily, my wife. And these here girls are my trusted Mountain Lions," he added, turning to the girls.

All four girls were wearing black jackets with their last names stitched in gold and a mountain lion logo under the words Mountain Lion. I remembered the driver—now standing beside me with two black trash bags she must've picked up from Vanity's—mentioning how it was thirty degrees cooler up here in the mountains than in the city we'd just left.

I fiddled with the ties on one of the trash bags, trying to channel the nervous energy building in my chest. Everyone was a little too close, too chipper. Their big smiles made the whole welcome feel rehearsed. Fake.

"Welcome to Mingus Mountain," Dave said proudly, sweeping his hand toward the scenery behind him.

One of the Mountain Lion girls started pointing to various buildings on the property, naming them off and telling me what each one was for. The tour I didn't ask for.

"This is the main building. It has thirty beds, a library, a main hall where some of the girls hang out during downtime, and the cafeteria—everyone eats here no matter what dorm they live in. The director's office and some of the other staff like the therapist are upstairs," she said, pausing to catch her breath. "We won't have time tonight for a full tour since it'll be dark soon, but tomorrow after breakfast I'll show you around and introduce you to the rest of the staff."

Apparently satisfied with her little rundown, the director and the other three girls left. I heard the tires of the van crunching on gravel as the driver headed back down the mountain.

I followed the girl—Pamela, I think—down the hallway of the massive two-story building. A few girls passed us, eyeing me with curiosity. It's always the same in a new place. Who's the new girl? What did she do to end up here? I gave them a half-smile and kept moving, struggling to keep hold of the two trash bags full of my clothes.

We turned off the main hall into the common area Pamela had mentioned. It reminded me of a game room—cozy couches, card tables, and folding chairs scattered around. Girls were spread out doing their own thing. Some watched TV, others read, a few whispered in corners.

About halfway down the hall, we stopped. This was it. My new room. My new life—probably until I turned eighteen.

Ugh.

"This is your room," she said. "Go ahead and unpack and settle in. I'll come get you just before dinner."

I nodded and stepped into the room with my bags, wondering if what she said meant I wasn't allowed to leave until she came back. There was a lot I still had to figure out about this place—and how things worked up here on this mountain.

The room featured a full-sized bathroom with a walk-in shower, double sinks, a clear mirror you could actually see your reflection in, and a porcelain toilet. After living in a 12-by-10 cell for several months with a three-in-one toilet, a tattered cot, and cold showers, this was more than an upgrade. The room itself was a decent size, with a walk-in closet, two dressers, a desk, and a bunk bed— with still plenty of floor space to move around.

There was already a girl—my new roommate—napping on the bottom bunk, which meant I'd be taking the top by default.

I had no idea which of my belongings from Vanity's house had made it into the black kitchen trash bags now sitting in the middle of the room. Part of me had absolutely no desire to go through them or put anything away, but I knew I wasn't going anywhere anytime soon. Might as well settle in.

I grabbed the bags and tore at the plastic until they ripped open, spilling the contents across the floor. The noise woke my roommate. She rolled over, looking at me and the mess I'd just made.

"Sorry," I said, giving her a weak smile.

"It's fine," she muttered, already rolling back over. "Wake me up when it's time for dinner."

"Mm, okay."

***

"Are we not allowed to enter each other's rooms?" I asked my guide when she returned to escort me to dinner. I noticed she hadn't actually stepped into my room—either when she brought me earlier or now. She stayed just outside the doorway.

"No. Going into a room that isn't assigned to you will get you in trouble."

"I see."

"I'm sure there are lots of reasons, but mostly because girls steal."

"Right," I said. I knew all about that from living in shelters and group homes.

"So, it just keeps things simple and makes it easier to track our movements in the building."

I hadn't thought to look for cameras before, but now I noticed them in the top corners of the hallways.

"Who watches the cameras?" I asked.

"I don't really know if anyone just sits and watches them all day. I think they mostly review footage if something happens," she said over her shoulder as she climbed the stairs to the cafeteria.

A long line had already formed with girls waiting to get their dinner. I picked up a brown tray and stood behind my guide, waiting my turn for whatever dinner would be.

The cafeteria was huge, taking up most of the upstairs floor space and giving the dining hall a lot of room to spread out. Plastic tables had been pushed together to form one giant rectangle in the center of the room.

When I got to the serving counter, I learned quickly that you had to take whatever was being served—whether you planned to eat it or not—unless you had a special diet. I didn't. I held my tray out as a kitchen helper scooped chicken, mashed potatoes, and corn onto it.

"After we eat dinner, we have Guided Group Intervention," my guide said between bites. I wanted to ask what that even was, but figured I'd learn soon enough. No point in interrupting.

"GGI can last a while," she continued, "so depending on how long it goes, we either go straight to bed or have a little downtime." I nodded as I chewed a bite of chicken.

"Girls usually use that time to shower, do homework, or just hang out until lights out."

"When is lights out?"

"9 p.m. That's when our doors are closed and we're not supposed to leave our rooms until morning staff comes in."

After dinner, staff asked all the girls to gather in the downstairs common area and sit in a circle on the floor. I found a spot next to my guide as more girls filed in and sat down. I noticed that the staff didn't sit in the circle with us—they sat outside it, in chairs. The three girls I'd met earlier when I arrived were already seated, still wearing their black Mountain Lion jackets.

"We have a new arrival with us today," one of the Mountain Lions said. "Nicole, would you like to introduce yourself to the group?"

"Hi, my name is Nicole," I said just above a whisper, not liking being put on the spot.

"Yes," she said, smiling. "Is there anything else you want to share with the group?"

I scanned the faces of the girls in the circle, all of them looking at me with quiet anticipation.

"No," I replied. It was too long of a story, really—because it wasn't just one thing that landed me in this therapeutic behavioral health facility.

The rest of the group session—ran entirely by the Mountain Lions—involved going around the circle while the girls spoke about their day and called each other out on unacceptable behaviors. I guess if someone wasn't following directions or was off-task, one of her peers was expected to reprimand her. Staff only stepped in if things escalated into a fight. Otherwise, the Mountain Lions ran their respective dorms.

In all the placements I'd been in, I'd never encountered a child-led environment with staff just observing. I wasn't sure I liked it, either. Being told what to do and how to act by out-of-touch adults was already bad enough—now I'd be bossed around by my peers too?

I watched as two girls went back and forth, airing out their beef from earlier in the day. My eyes darted between them like I was watching a verbal ping pong match, both entertained and uncomfortable. People frustrate me. They do and say things I don't like all the time. But the idea of confronting someone head-on, of actually voicing my grievances, makes me a bundle of nerves. I guess I'd rather take the passive-aggressive route than be assertive and direct.

I was relieved when Guided Group Intervention finally ended and dreaded knowing it would happen twice a day. I lay on the top bunk, waiting for my nerves to settle from all the day's activity and for sleep to come.

Surprisingly, my sleep was restful, and I woke up feeling refreshed. On top of my dresser were three neatly folded red shirts. I climbed down to inspect them and saw they said Mingus Mountain across the chest.

"What are these?" I asked my roommate.

"It's our school uniform. Everyone has to wear one."

"Are there different colors for different levels?" I asked, wondering if it was a system like juvenile detention.

"No. Everyone wears red shirts. When you become a Mountain Lion—which is the final step of the program—you get a jacket with your name on it."

"Is it easy to become a Mountain Lion? How come you aren't one yet?"

"Everyone has their own program and goals to meet. It just takes time, I guess."

"Based on what I saw last night, they're a bunch of know-it-all do-gooders acting like adults." She didn't reply. I started to wonder if the program had already brainwashed her into thinking kids bossing around other kids was normal. "How long have you been here?" I asked, switching the subject.

"About a year. I have a meeting with the higher-ups in a couple of weeks to be promoted to Mountain Lion."

So, I had just insulted her.

Thankfully, Pamela—my guide—showed up at the door before things got any more awkward between us.

"So, you're just going to shadow me today until staff prints your schedule."

"Sounds good," I said.

***

A week passed before I got my own schedule and no longer needed a guide to take me from place to place around the large campus. I met Bonnie, a weathered woman who took care of the 17 horses and two dogs, and Harvey, a thin man with a ponytail and long beard who served as both the PE and hiking instructor.

All the buildings were stand-alone and fairly spread out, making me more physically active than I had ever been in my life. The school was on one peak of the mountain, the chapel on another. The gym had its own building, as did each of the three dorms, and the director and his wife had a separate house as well.

Most days, I spent my free time alone on my top bunk, reading the books I checked out from the library. I had never been good at sports, nor did I care much for physical activity. So instead of joining the others, I sat against the wall and watched the girls play basketball in the courtyard.

Three months went by before I was told that this was a problem—that keeping to myself was considered isolating behavior. I had been quietly pulled out of art class—one of my favorites—for a progress report meeting I didn't even know was happening.

In attendance: the resident therapist, two of the evening staff, the director and his wife, and my case manager. The room was just an open space with a long conference table in the middle and a phone placed at the center. I found myself staring at it, wondering if the room was monitored, or if maybe I could sneak up here during downtime and make a call.

So far, the only phones I'd seen in the entire place were in the staff offices—locked behind doors when not in use. Even in classrooms, the phones sat on the teachers' desks and those rooms were always locked too.

"As far as behavior goes," the director began, "I haven't heard anything negative. She seems to be adjusting well."

I finally tore my eyes away from the phone, a flicker of hope rising. Maybe this meant something. Maybe my caseworker would reconsider my placement. Maybe I could go back to Phoenix. She could figure out whatever mess Vivian had created and force her to honor the visitation she promised. There had to be a way to hold her accountable.

"Yes, Nicole hasn't had any behavior issues since arriving," Shelby, one of the evening staff, added. "But I feel she's been antisocial, and that's concerning."

I looked at her in disbelief. Is she joking? Who the hell cares how social I am?

"I like reading," I said, glaring at her, my tone sharp with annoyance. "Why is that concerning?"

"In my experience, isolating can lead to depression—if it's not already a sign of depression."

"I'm not depressed," I said flatly. Technically? Maybe I was. But how would she know that? And why did it matter if I wasn't causing any issues? What were they even planning to do about it?

"I think it would be beneficial if Nicole starts having weekly meetings with the therapist," she said, glancing toward the man I now realized was the therapist.

A therapist. If they actually cared, they'd reunite me with my child—the child they forced me to hand over for adoption. And now they want to offer therapy?

"Hi, Nicole. My name is Parker," he said with a smile.

I looked away, refusing to acknowledge him.

I just couldn't win with these people. If it wasn't one thing, it was another. Let me get this straight: I was sent away to a mountain because I was labeled incorrigible, a danger to myself, and a safety risk for the state. No one cared how I was coping with postpartum. No one thought about what it meant to be yanked from my baby, weaned cold turkey, shoved back into school, and then locked up without ever seeing him again—even with an open adoption agreement.

None of that mattered.

But now that I'm behaving? Now that I'm not a problem? Now it's a problem—and I need therapy?

"So… I need to make friends?" I asked, voice dry.

She smiled. "I can't say whether the connections you make here will turn into friendships. But making healthy connections is important."

Escape

Normally, I was starving before lunchtime—snacks were never a thing in here—and I couldn't wait to eat. But after that meeting, I couldn't even stomach the thought of food. I sat in the cafeteria, picking at my tray and scanning the girls, trying to figure out who I could possibly see myself engaging with.

The ones who were always having some kind of emotional breakdown or loud, unstable outburst? Definitely not. I had enough emotions of my own to manage without trying to figure out what demons someone else was battling.

Then there were the do-gooder Mountain Lions and the kiss-asses desperately trying to get into their little club. Also no. Ick.

That left Crystal and Asha.

Crystal wasn't weird exactly, just… unusual. She had this extremely rare medical condition that made her body metabolize sugar into alcohol. Yeah—actual alcohol. Apparently, she used to break her sugar-free diet on purpose to get drunk. Her parents sent her here for that. Honestly, I felt bad for her. A sugar-free existence? That sounded like hell. And to be sent away over it, by your own parents? They even paid cash for her placement. I guess they had money—she was from Napa Valley, California. If I had parents, and they did something like that to me, I'd never forgive them.

Asha was the total opposite of Crystal. Where Crystal was bubbly and sweet, Asha gave off a quiet, shadowy vibe—like a modern-day Wednesday Addams, but with a better name. Pale skin, long curly black hair that always parted perfectly down the middle, and an even quieter presence than mine.

Crystal and I were too different to ever really bond. The only thing we had in common was that our birthdays were a few days apart. We were both Capricorns—me in December, her in January. Still, sitting next to her during meals was pleasant enough. Her energy was light, and conversation was easy.

But Asha? Sitting near her at night before bed, when we all had to look like we were socializing, wasn't bad. She didn't ask too many questions, and we both preferred silence.

"I really want to get out of here," Asha mumbled one night, her head resting on her knees.

"Who are you telling?"

"I heard this one girl tried to run away a few years ago," she said, lifting her head to look at me. "Stole a van and everything."

"No way."

"Yeah. Staff said she stole keys, actually drove the van. But I guess she didn't know what she was doing and pulled over once they caught up to her."

"That's wild," I said, eyes wide.

"Right? I wonder how she even got the keys. I can't figure out how to use any of the phones here."

"Who do you even want to call?"

I hadn't told anyone here about my baby. I didn't want to go there.

"I want to try and get ahold of my old foster mom," I said vaguely.

"I bet if I got to a phone, my boyfriend would come get us."

That night I lay in bed, wide awake, thinking about everything Asha had said. Was she serious? Because if she was, we'd need a real plan. And it couldn't involve stealing a van—we'd never pull that off. Every room here locked automatically when staff walked out. Clearly, they'd learned their lesson from the last escape attempt.

If we were going to get off this mountain, we'd have to hike.

The next day, I went about my business as usual. No sudden changes. No odd behavior. I didn't want to draw attention to myself.

After dinner, I found Asha sitting in a corner of the common room near the fireplace, curled up in a hooded sweater like she was trying to disappear.

I sat down next to her and leaned in.

"I thought about it," I whispered. "If we're going to do this, we'll have to hike down. I don't know how to drive. Do you?"

She shook her head. "No."

"Okay, so… we'd leave after school, before dinner, during free hour. It's the only time no one's really checking for us."

"Yeah."

I narrowed my eyes at her. "Yeah, like—you really want to do this? You think your boyfriend could meet us at the freeway?"

"Yeah," she said again, steady and sure.

I nodded and stood up from the fireplace.

"Tomorrow then?"

"Tomorrow."

School seemed to last forever. I watched the clock all day, mentally preparing for me and Asha's escape off this mountain. I knew I wouldn't be able to bring much with me—just water, really—because walking down the hill with a backpack full of clothes would be way too suspect.

No, the plan was to go back to the dorm, change out of the school uniform, and put on regular clothes. Jeans, a T-shirt, and boots. I didn't have hiking boots, but that didn't have to be a problem. The boots I had had a low enough heel and came up to my shin. That would be enough to keep the pokies and brush from tearing up my socks and ankles as I hiked.

I hadn't really figured out what came after Asha's boyfriend picked us up. Maybe just show up at Vanity's house and demand she have her daughter bring me my son. But first things first—get off this mountain.

I changed quickly and went looking for Asha. It didn't take long. She was a creature of habit and always in the same two spots. I sat down next to her and noticed she'd already changed into her usual oversized hoodie, sweatpants, and sneakers.

"Are you ready to leave? We can stop in the kitchen and grab water on the way out."

"I decided I'm not going to leave."

"What? This was your idea."

"I know. I just want to stay sober… and if I leave, I know I'll relapse."

"Seriously?" I said, standing up and fuming. Why hadn't I seen this coming? All the girls here had something—some emotional spiral, some drug issue. Even sweet Crystal, who literally let her body turn sugar into alcohol on purpose. I was surrounded by mentally weak-minded people.

"Fine. You stay. You probably need this place anyway. I'm leaving."

There were no girls in the cafeteria when I got upstairs, which worked in my favor. I grabbed two bottles of water—the most I could carry without a bag—and slipped out the back door. My heart was racing, adrenaline pouring through me. I had no idea what my plan was beyond getting away, but I was committed now.

I walked quickly down the steps leading outside and rounded the building. I didn't have far to go before the slope started, and once I got there, I looked around several times to make sure no one was out and about. Turns out I picked the best time to leave—even the two dogs were distracted.

Getting down the first slope was easy. Once I made it past that, I started to relax a little. I just had to keep moving at a steady pace.

I'd gone on hikes and trail rides before on the weekends with the hiking instructor, but those were always on well-worn paths. This wasn't that. Now I was carving my own trail, keeping an eye out for jumping cholla—cactus with thin, razor-sharp spines that, if you so much as brushed against them, would barb deep into your skin.

Other things were in the back of my mind—mountain lions, coyotes, javelinas, snakes. Snakes were actually more front of mind. While mountain lions were supposedly common in these mountains, I'd never seen one or even heard of a student or staff spotting one. Coyotes and javelinas, on the other hand—I had seen those.

There'd been one time I watched a lone coyote not far from the dorms. Staff said it was probably just hungry and thirsty and more scared of me than I was of it. I saw it walk right into the horse encampment. The entire herd of horses just moved to the other side of the enclosure while the coyote helped itself to some pellets and water, then left the same way it came. Honestly, the two dogs around here caused more trouble for the horses than that wild coyote ever did.

While I had also seen javelinas, I hadn't viewed them as much of a threat either.

No.

My real concern was the snakes I would soon be unable to see—especially the rattlesnakes. I might hear one, but by then it would already be too close for me to escape. Still, unwilling to turn back, I shoved even the thought of snakes to the back of my mind and kept hiking swiftly down.

The sun had begun to set, making me second-guess my decision all over again. Maybe I could abort the mission, slip back into the dorms, and no one would be any wiser that I had left in the first place. I turned to look back, trying to see how far I'd come, but because of the slopes and dips in the mountain terrain, I couldn't even see the top where I'd started. I guessed I'd been hiking for a couple of hours. It had to be dinner time—or close to it.

With darkness creeping in, I started veering diagonally to get closer to the road. The same road I'd been driven down months ago when they brought me to this place. I figured if I could follow it down without being seen, I might actually make it. Once I was discovered missing, I knew they'd send staff to search. I had to be close enough to follow the road… but far enough not to be caught.

As I neared the road, I took another swig from my water bottle and saw I had maybe an inch left. I was parched from practically jogging down the mountain, but if I finished this one, I'd be down to my last bottle—and I had no clue how much further I still had to go.

It was pitch black by the time I saw the headlights of the white van creeping down the road. With no water left, feet aching, body cold and exhausted, I actually felt annoyed that they couldn't see me—when I could see them perfectly. The fact that they just assumed I'd be walking directly on the road to get caught? Insulting. They didn't even shine a flashlight into the trees or brush. Like, hello? If I had stayed on the road, I'd have been found in minutes. And the idea that they thought I was that dumb, that I didn't have even that much sense or drive to pull this off—it was actually offensive.

Eventually, I made it off the mountain and reached the two-lane freeway. Thirsty, freezing, and exhausted after hiking for hours, fear started creeping in. Scenes from Freeway and Joy Ride flashed through my head, and I couldn't stop my imagination from spiraling. Any one of these truckers could be a serial killer, just waiting for a naive, desperate teen runaway to make their night.

I sprinted across the freeway to the southbound side and immediately started feeling stupid. What was my plan, really? I had no money. No phone. No way to contact anyone. No ride into Phoenix. The idea of hitchhiking—now that I was actually standing here—felt insane. That would be my death, for sure.

I had been so mad at Asha for backing out of our half-baked escape plan, I got stubborn. I left anyway, fueled by anger more than logic. But now that I was here—alone, in the desert, on the side of some forgotten highway—I realized I hadn't thought it through. Not the cold. Not the dehydration. Not the pimps, serial killers, or the vast nothingness between here and the next place. Not even the dark.

Not wanting to make myself an easy target, I stepped off the freeway and into the desert. Not far, just enough to avoid being directly in anyone's line of sight. But there were no streetlamps out here. I was in total darkness except for the occasional car or semi-truck flying by, their headlights slicing through the night. Each time one passed, I dropped low, ducking out of instinct—terrified of being spotted, abducted, sex-trafficked, or worse. Thrown in a dungeon to die. Okay, maybe not a dungeon… more like a basement. Either way—dead.

I kept tripping, my feet catching on rocks and tangled brush I couldn't see.

I knew I was dehydrated. I couldn't keep going like this. My body was screaming.

I collapsed just off the side of the road, still making every effort to remain hidden from any car or truck that sped by. It was time for me to throw in the towel and wait to be found. At this point, I was going to die from either dehydration and cold… or murder.

I started paying closer attention to the vehicles as they passed, trying to spot the Mingus Mountain van. The fear of stepping out too soon and waving down the wrong van kept me frozen. I needed to be sure. I needed to flag down the right van—the one that would take me back to food, water, and heat. The one that would bring me back to safety.

But every vehicle that passed was just a semi-truck or a car.

Had they stopped looking for me?

Maybe they thought I'd already made it to a gas station. Maybe they assumed I'd hitched a ride. Or worse—they'd simply given up for the night. It was late, and if I was tired, they must be too. They probably figured they'd find me in the morning when it was light out. The most horrifying part? That might not even be out of laziness—it might just be the policy. I'd only seen the white van once, hours ago, when I was still up on the damn mountain.

I had no blanket. No food. No water. No flashlight. And a real, pulsing fear of being kidnapped. I realized I didn't want to sleep in the desert off the side of the freeway. I needed them to find me.

When I finally spotted the white van again, I stepped out from where I'd been crouched and started waving both arms until I was seen. The van stopped just past me, then slowly reversed until it was right beside me. I heard the door unlock and I didn't hesitate—I slid it open and climbed inside.

Thankfully, the heat was already blasting. I climbed into the back and spotted a bottle of water on the seat. I didn't know if it had been left there for me or just forgotten from an off-site activity, but I opened it immediately and took a sip. My throat was so raw it hurt to swallow that first gulp.

The ride back up the mountain was silent. And I was fine with that.

When we arrived, I was walked directly to the office and told to sit. No one yelled. No one even addressed what I had done. And somehow, that was more unnerving than if they'd screamed at me.

Marlene, the head staff, typed something on her computer. I heard a printer start up. Then the phone rang.

"Hello," she said into the receiver. "Yes, we found her." She let out a chuckle. "Better yet, she waved us down." More laughter. "You should've seen the condition we found her in. Did you know she was wearing thigh-high boots? With a heel?"

Her gaze landed on me again, sweeping over my disheveled, cold, hungry frame.

They weren't mad because they thought I was the dumbest person alive. And to them, that was funny.

Briana, the other night staffer, was laughing now too. She and Marlene chatted back and forth like I wasn't even in the room. And as exhausted as I was, I wondered why I wasn't just allowed to go to bed. Maybe this was my punishment—sleep deprivation and a heavy dose of shame.

"How could you think two bottles of water was enough?" they mocked. "No jacket? No food? What was your plan?"

They weren't wrong. What had my plan been?

Especially since every other time I ran away back in Phoenix—or anywhere close to it—something bad always happened.

I thought about saying something. Maybe asking to go to the kitchen to get a snack. But I couldn't bring myself to interrupt their laughter as they filled out the incident report. Instead, I sat there quietly, trying to distract myself with anything in the tiny office. I squinted at the spine of a book on the shelf. Studied the degrees Marlene had framed on the wall behind her. Tried to make out what she was writing about me on the form.

Morning came fast, probably because I was already well into it by the time I was finally walked back to my unit. I had no desire to get up and out of bed. For starters, my legs were stiff and sore—but more than that, I had zero interest in facing the ridicule I knew was coming, or sitting through lectures from the do-gooder Mountain Lions.

I passed Asha in the hallway but couldn't even look at her.

I didn't want anyone to look at me. Or speak to me. But I knew I wouldn't be able to avoid it forever.

Staff had accused me of isolating months ago, and while they might've been wrong then, they were absolutely right now. I had every intention of isolating from my peers. Starting today.

I was last in line for breakfast, doing my best to avoid eye contact. I sat at the far end table, ate fast, and dreaded the inevitable: guided group intervention.

Word traveled fast. Even the teacher knew. The damn hiking instructor. The horse instructor. All of them heard about my "pointless excursion" through the desert—with no jacket, no food, the wrong shoes, and just two bottles of water.

I flopped down on the cold gym floor and crossed my legs, already knowing I'd be the only topic of conversation today, no matter what drama the other girls had brewing. This was their moment to shine—to prove they were "working the program" and would never do something as reckless. To talk about my "poor choices" and how "concerned" they were. Bullshit.

None of it would be real.

First of all, every girl in this place was asleep during my escape. And I'm sure they all went to bed early because of it. So miss me with the concern. Second, they were all just parroting what they thought the responsible, well-adjusted adults wanted to hear. The kinds of adults who'd grown up with stability. Love. A functioning life.

I sat and listened, because I had no choice. I tried to hide how annoyed I was as girl after girl repeated what the last one said.

Hello?

Did you not just hear what she said two seconds ago?

Goodness.

Did every single one of them need to speak?

"I know what I did was reckless." I forced the words out, knowing if I didn't apologize and feign remorse, the lecture would drag on longer. I'd seen it happen too many times—girls who stayed quiet or got defensive just made things worse for themselves. "I have every intention of working the program."

I wasn't even lying.

What other choice did I have?

The way I saw it, I'd be seventeen at the end of the year. They couldn't keep me past eighteen anyway. As a ward of the state, I'd learned how to pick my battles. When to give up the fight. When to go along just enough to survive.

Prescott was my reality. Mingus Mountain would be my residence until I aged out, and my social worker finally came to take me off this mountain.

Aged Out

The days began to blur together until the staff—and everyone else involved in my case plan—finally agreed: I had successfully completed my program on the mountain.

Classic "if you can't beat them, join them." I couldn't beat them. I had tried. So I started going on the local hikes, even the all-day weekend ones. I joined the trail rides, participated in group activities, threw a basketball here and there when the girls were playing. I read a little less and showed up a little more. Played along long enough to earn myself a Mountain Lion jacket—black, with a picture of a lion stretched across the chest.

Once I was back in Phoenix, I reached out to Vanity. I was 18 now, and I had no one and nowhere else to go. She'd moved since I last saw her—from Maryvale to the distant suburbs of Goodyear. A new build with fresh paint, new appliances, and every inch of it filled with her many things. I helped her around the house when she needed—which was always. Go get this, clean that, help here, do that. And when I wasn't helping, I was tucked away in the spare bedroom she let me use.

Vanity didn't seem to mind me being there, and for me, she was the devil I knew. She was the closest person to my son. I needed her. I needed to stay on her good side. So I kept my head down and stayed in my lane. My lane was waiting for crumbs—like a photo of my son, handed over when she felt like it.

One time, it was a picture of Vivian holding him in front of an Easter Bunny backdrop. I hated it. Hated her.

Mother's Day made things worse. Her family had a gathering planned, and of course, I wasn't invited. It stung. But I had to pretend I didn't care. I had to act like being shut out didn't hurt, because if I let that hurt show, Vanity might cut me off entirely. Vivian wasn't speaking to me. My son's whereabouts, despite him living under her roof, remained a mystery. I asked about him. Vanity said he was fine. That he was smart. That he was doing well. That was it.

Charles came by Vanity's house sometimes to visit me. For my son's birthday, he bought a toy truck. I gave it to Vanity to pass along, but I don't believe it ever made it to Vivian's house. After that, Vanity started acting funny. Complaining about me being there.

"I need you to get a job and start contributing. You can't just live here for free."

And to be fair, I really wasn't doing much. I didn't have a license, let alone a car. I didn't even have a GED or diploma. I spent most of my time in my room watching TV, riding around in Charles's car or chilling in whatever hotel room he got. When I wasn't doing that, I was on the phone chat lines.

It was the phone chat lines that led me into one of the scariest situations of my life—being held captive in Las Vegas.

I'd met a man on there. We hit it off. Exchanged numbers. He invited me to Vegas. I was a fool and said yes, thinking he was interested in a real relationship. I don't even know how long I was stuck there. Eventually, I escaped—ran out into the freezing night in nothing but a jumpsuit. I made it to a corner store and begged for help.

Two guys were outside. I walked up to them.

"Can you take me to the Greyhound?" I asked.

"Nah," one of them said. "I'll give you a ride, but not to the Greyhound, shawty. I don't got gas for all that."

I didn't have gas either. Hell, I didn't even have pockets. "Where y'all headed?" I asked, knowing I couldn't keep standing outside in the cold.

"Just back to the crib."

"Can I come?" I asked.

He looked me over from head to toe.

"Yeah," he said. "Get in."

We don't drive too far before we pull up at his house. Inside, it looks like maybe the house actually belongs to his grandmother, and he just lives with her. There's low brown carpet and flower-patterned furniture. He leads me straight to the back of the house, past the kitchen. I want to ask if he has any food I can have, but I go back and forth in my head—does he even have food? Would he give me any? Maybe he'll just offer?

But then we're already past the kitchen and in his room.

I sit on the bed. His room is a total boy's room—shoes thrown everywhere, dirty socks near the hamper but not in it. He's got a big TV on his dresser with a game console hooked up. He's busy messing with the DVD player when his friend walks in and plops down on the bed too.

He turns to ask me something but never finishes the sentence—because I'm suddenly throwing up all over him.

He jumps back, yelling, disgusted. "Gross. What the fuck?!"

His friend hops up too. "Damn, girl, you sick or something?"

I wasn't sick. I had no idea why I had just thrown up on him and all over the floor. I jump up, frantically apologizing.

"I'm so sorry. Let me clean it up—"

He leaves the room and comes back with cleaning supplies.

"How about you just go sit on the couch," he says, annoyed. "Don't throw up on anything else. I'll call a friend to take you to the Greyhound."

I sit on the couch, staring at the black TV screen, realizing that the car must not have been either of theirs. Probably his grandma's. And for whatever reason, he didn't—or couldn't—drive it to the Greyhound.

A few hours go by before he finally finds someone willing to give me a ride. I end up standing at the Greyhound station counter, asking if I can use their phone. I call Charles.

"Can you come pick me up?"

"Sure. Where are you at?"

"I'm at the Greyhound. In Vegas." I hold my breath.

"Just stay there. I'm coming to get you. It'll be about five hours though."

"Thanks," I say, taking a seat in the big waiting area.

I watch people come and go. Boarding buses. Getting off them. Meeting loved ones. Eating snacks I can't afford. Cokes from the vending machine cost $1.25 and I don't even have that.

When Charles finally makes it from Phoenix to the Greyhound in Vegas, I'm beyond grateful.

He was my savior. My knight in shining armor. I loved him. I thought he loved me too—until I got pregnant.

Before the pregnancy though, he really was great.

Yep. I was pregnant again.

I looked up to Charles. I adored him. After Vanity made a fuss about me not having a job or contributing, Charles took me to an interview. He co-signed on my studio apartment after I moved out of Vanity's. The same apartment I live in now.

But everything changed when I got pregnant. He got angry. Told me it wasn't possible. I wasn't 15 anymore—I was 18—and I damn well understood how pregnancy happens.

Turned out Charles was married. Had an 8-year-old daughter. That was why I "couldn't possibly" be pregnant. My pregnancy stirred up issues with his wife.

Delusion had me thinking he was choosing me. After everything he'd done for me, after showing up for me in some of my darkest moments, I thought he was mine. But he wasn't.

Suddenly, he stopped showing up at all. He never went to a single doctor's appointment. He accused me of cheating and wanted to break up.

I didn't accept the breakup. I tried to win him back. Tried to make him choose me. Tried to make him care about the son we were about to have.

After my anatomy scan, I sent him an instant message: "It's a boy."

That got a response.

Lately, he'd been ignoring my messages or sending dry, one-word replies. But when I told him it was a boy, he lit up a little.

And I ran with it.

What should we name him? I typed into the computer, excited that he was finally showing interest in the pregnancy.

Something starting with a C, he replied.

I sat at my small Walmart computer desk, staring at the screen, trying to think of C names.

Chauncy, I typed back.

No.

Okay. I tried again.

Chris.

No.

C names weren't coming to me. I tried again.

Clyde. I actually really liked that one. Clyde felt like a cool, laid-back kind of name. A chill dude.

No.

I sighed.

Okay, then what name?

Charles.

Charles? I typed, confused. That's your name.

I know.

So… he'll be a junior? I asked. I didn't exactly love the idea, but I was too happy that he was finally talking to me to push back.

Well actually, he'll be the third.

Huh. That was actually kind of cool. A name passed down. A tradition. Something permanent. I could get on board with that.

Charles it is, I typed back. Should he have a middle name?

James.

His exact name.

I agreed to it. Not because I was fully on board, but because it felt like maybe—just maybe—I had his attention now. Like he was starting to care. Maybe naming the baby meant something.

But he kept skipping doctor's appointments. I tried not to take it personally. Told myself it didn't really mean anything. People said men don't really feel like fathers until they see the baby. Until they're holding an actual human life in their arms.

He still had a few months.

Vital Records

I looked at the clock on the microwave in the small studio apartment Charles had helped me get.

Now seven months pregnant, I was always starving. At work, there were only a few overpriced vending machines, and everything inside was loaded with sodium or sugar. I had been trying to keep a decent enough diet for my unborn son.

12:36.

Just enough time to microwave a frozen Stouffer's lasagna and eat it before leaving for work.

My shift didn't actually start until 3 p.m., but I had to take two buses to get there—two extremely long hours just to commute. I guess I should've felt lucky to have even gotten the job. The grocery store across the street and the fast-food place just off to the side both required a high school diploma or GED. I had neither. Just Charles, who made sure I got hired.

I stared at the microwave as the timer counted down the last few minutes of my breakfast when my phone started to jingle.

Vanity's number flashed across the screen.

I hurried to press the green icon.

I hadn't spoken to her since I left her house months ago. As much as her indifference annoyed my soul, I had tried to make small talk—asked about Vivian and my son's whereabouts. She had been pleasant enough, telling me only that she'd moved. But when I asked where, she would suddenly need to go. So seeing her number now, out of nowhere, was a shock.

"Hello?" I answered, more like a question than a greeting.

For a moment, I let myself hope that maybe she was calling because she finally felt guilty. Maybe she was ready to stop helping her daughter hide my son.

"Hi, Nicole. How have you been?"

How have I been? I rolled my eyes just as the microwave dinged.

"Oh, I'm great," I said, not even trying to hide the annoyance in my voice. I still didn't know why she had called, but that overly sweet tone told me she was going to ask for something. I'd heard it a hundred times when she needed something from a man—this fake sugary sweetness. And now, she was using it on me.

"I just wanted to let you know Jayshawn is doing really well. He's such a smart and happy child."

What the hell?

I pulled the phone away from my ear to double-check that this was real, that I was on an actual call.

She was just casually making small talk about the child she helped keep away from me—as if we were talking about our favorite movie character or something.

"Oh," I said, unable to think of a better response.

"Yes! He's ready to start preschool," she added, her voice full of excitement. I didn't know if she thought she was being generous by "sharing" these little facts with me or if she was trying to taunt me. Either way, the anger started rising in my chest. My appetite for the cheesy lasagna disappeared instantly.

"I wanted to know if you could get me a copy of his birth certificate for Vivian?"

Ah. There it was.

So she did want something.

Why in the world she thought I would do a favor for her lying, backstabbing daughter was beyond me. At least now I knew what this little charade was about.

"You want to know if I can get Vivian a copy of Jayshawn's birth certificate?" I repeated slowly.

"So she can enroll him in preschool," she said lightly. "Yes."

My mind started racing.

Replaying the day I gave birth. The immediate days after. The court dates. The paperwork.

Because the only way I would be able to get a copy of Jayshawn's birth certificate… is if I was still legally his mother.

If my parental rights hadn't been terminated.

If he had never actually been adopted.

And that fact I knew for sure.

When I applied for my $8.50-an-hour call center job, the name on the birth certificate wasn't mine.

My mother's name wasn't on it either.

The name that appeared on my birth certificate was the name of the woman who had adopted me and my sister—Patricia—and her husband, Elton.

Even the name Myisha—the one given to me by the woman who birthed me, my biological mother—didn't appear on the current and only legally accepted copy of my birth certificate.

Instead, the name listed was Nicole.

Because when a child is adopted, a new birth certificate is created. The new parents' names are added, and the old document is replaced. The state, in essence, falsifies birth records.

Sometimes, like in my case, the adoptive parents take it a step further and change the child's name entirely.

I remember the woman from Vital Records coming into the hospital room.

She spoke to me directly.

I try to recall any other details—her name, the conversation, what I signed— but nothing significant comes to mind.

She left the room, and shortly after that, I was discharged.

Before I left Vivian's house to return to Vanity's around the start of the school year, I'd signed something at a bank that needed to be notarized. For years, I believed that was the adoption paperwork. But now… I wasn't so sure.

It might have been something else entirely.

"Yes," I finally said aloud, realizing I had been staring blankly at my plate, lost in thought, and hadn't actually answered Vanity's question.

"Where is Vivian living now?" I asked, keeping my tone neutral.

Vanity took a long pause—clearly deciding how much was too much to tell me.

"Mesa," she finally said, like the word physically hurt her.

Of course.

The bare minimum. Again.

It was complete bullshit that she was helping conceal Jayshawn's whereabouts from me.

But if he had never actually been adopted, that might explain everything.

I needed to investigate—and I needed to do it immediately.

"Oh, wow. Well, I'm in Phoenix," I replied, offering information she didn't ask for. "I don't have a car, so once I get the birth certificate, I'll give you a call and you can pick it up."

A lie.

She would never be hearing from me again.

***

Here goes nothing.

If I could get a copy of my son's birth certificate, I would know—without a doubt—that he was never legally adopted.

I pushed open the doors of Vital Records and stepped inside.

From a red plastic dispenser attached to the wall, I pulled ticket number 56 and found a seat.

An hour passed before I finally heard my number called.

"Good morning," a clerk greeted me through a speaker in the middle of the thick, tempered glass.

"How can I help you?"

"I need a copy of my son's birth certificate," I said, sliding the paperwork I'd filled out through the small slot in the glass.

"Driver's license or ID?"

I dug through my purse until I found my ID and passed it through the same opening.

I watched her nervously as she typed into the computer. I knew I wasn't committing a crime by asking for a document I might not have legal access to. At worst, they'd just say no and move on to the next number.

Still, I couldn't stop shifting in my seat.

"Alrighty," she said, finally smiling. "That'll be $20. Cash or card?"

"Hmm." I rummaged again, pulling out a ten-dollar bill, a five, and four ones. I considered dumping my whole purse onto the counter. I had to have another dollar. Or four quarters.

"I'm sorry," I mumbled, giving the clerk a weak smile as I checked every pocket of my purse again.

Finally—I found a crumpled bill at the bottom and handed it over.

"Let me go print it off. I'll be right back," she said, stuffing the money into a drawer and walking away.

When she returned, I held the paper in my hands.

My son's birth certificate.

It was everything I had suspected.

Vivian never adopted him.

She pretended she had.

She kept him from me. Called the police on me when I skipped school to try and see him—had me locked in juvie.

And now, I held the proof.

The physical, legal proof of the lie. Of the betrayal.

Rage and adrenaline surged through me.

All the pain she had caused. The lies. The broken promises. The manipulation.

She promised I could be in my son's life.

She lied.

As I stepped out of Vital Records and into the sun, one thing was absolutely certain:

I was getting my son back from Vivian.

***

I have no clue what I am doing when I walk through the courthouse doors.

I stand in line behind people dressed in suits and various business-casual attire, feeling completely out of place as I wait my turn to go through the security checkpoint.

An information desk sits to the right of the checkpoint, with two women seated behind it.

I place my purse on the conveyor belt and hold my hands at my sides as I walk through the metal detector.

I don't know why metal detectors make me nervous. I have literally nothing on me—but I still feel guilty, like maybe I am hiding something security might find.

Without saying a word to me, I'm waved over to retrieve my items off the belt. I head straight to the information desk.

"How may I help you?"

How may they help me? I wonder.

I don't even know how to explain this situation.

Maybe they can't help me.

"I was told my son was adopted, but I learned he wasn't actually adopted, so I want him returned to me." I blurt it all out in one breath, hoping the woman can work with something I've said.

"So… you're looking to petition for custody of a minor?"

"Yes," I say, dragging it out.

"Okay. There are a bunch of computers over there that are free to use." She points to her right.

"And that sweet woman there"—she gestures toward an elderly woman with silver hair—"can help you fill out the paperwork."

I sit down at an open computer and read the instructions taped to the right side of the monitor.

Hovering the mouse over the Court Forms icon, I double-click.

A larger list opens, sorted into categories. Family Court seems like the right one.

The list is long, and I quickly scan a few:

Divorce with a Minor

Legal Separation with a Minor
Establish Paternity

Nothing fits my situation.

Filling out the wrong form won't help me.

"Excuse me," I call out to the silver-haired woman. "I don't think any of these forms fit my situation."

"What is it that you're looking for?"

"I want my child to be returned to me, but there's no divorce or separation or that type of thing. All these forms are about relationships ending, with a child caught in the middle."

"You'll need to fill out a Blank Motion Form."

She walks away and comes back with a file.

"Here you are."

I look at the five-page packet she hands me.

The top right corner is straightforward.

Person Filing:

I print my full name in small, neat handwriting.

Address. Phone Number. Email. Lawyer Bar Number.

I don't have a lawyer. I'm not a lawyer. I leave that part blank.

Below that, in smaller font, a prompt asks whether I'm representing myself without a lawyer, or if I'm an attorney filing on behalf of the petitioner or respondent.

I check the box for representing self.

I shouldn't need a lawyer.

Vivian never adopted my son like she said she would.

She is not his mother.

I am.

He should be returned to me.

A few spaces down, in bold capital letters, is the name of the courthouse:

Superior Court of Arizona in Maricopa County

Then a blank space:

Explain what you want the court to order. The judge may grant, deny, or change your request. A ruling will be issued by minute entry.

How much detail should I include?

I really only have space for about 150 words unless I write on the back of the page—and I don't want to do that.

My handwriting isn't neat enough to write freeform without lines.

So I write:

I am requesting Vivian return my son to me. We had an agreement that she would adopt him. The agreement was for an open adoption, however she never kept the terms, cutting off all ties with me a few months after his birth. I recently learned she had never legally adopted my son to begin with, so I am requesting she give him back.

I cap the pen and reread what I've written.

Then I stand up to look for the silver-haired woman and ask what to do next.

"You're going to go to the copier over there and print out three sets of copies."

"Three?"

"Yes. A copy for yourself, the respondent, and then a copy to file with the court.

Once you have your three copies, you're going to head over there and stand in line."

I head over to the copy machine and immediately have no clue what I'm doing. There are so many buttons, and none of them seem to mean copy. I don't even know where to put the paper in—there's just so much going on with this machine.

I watch as someone uses a similar copy machine next to me. They seem to have figured it out.

"Can you help me make a few copies?" I ask.

"You have to pay before they'll print," he says, walking off with zero interest in actually helping me.

I tinker with the machine some more before giving up and going back to the help desk.

"Can someone please help me with the copy machine?"

I seriously cannot be the only person who doesn't know how to use a commercial copy machine.

Finally, someone from the help center comes over and gets the copy machine to make three sets of forms. I head back over to the workstation I was at earlier and staple them together.

There's nobody ahead of me at the filing line, so I stand at the front, waiting to be motioned over by one of the court staff.

"Next," a woman straight across from me calls. "How can I help you?"

"I want to file this motion with the court, requesting to see a judge," I say, handing her the paperwork I just copied.

She takes what I have and stamps it.

"Do not forget—you need to send all parties copies of these filings via certified mail."

"So… I'm not sure of the respondent's current address because I don't know where she lives. But I do know her mother's address. So how does that work?"

"You'll need to send the forms to that last known address, and the person, once notified, has 30 days to respond."

"Thanks."

I start to exit the courthouse when I notice another copy machine not in use. Can't hurt to make one more copy of the paperwork and have it sent to Vanity's home address as well. She'll certainly notify her daughter that she's received mail—if she doesn't open it herself.

***

I was starting to think maybe Vivian hadn't responded back to the courts within the thirty-day time frame. I know Vanity got the court paperwork. She hadn't bothered reaching back out about the birth certificate either, and at this point—why would she?

Normally, I went weeks without checking my mail, but now I feel like I've become obsessed with walking down to the mailboxes, hoping to see if a judge will enforce my request.

I open the mailbox and pull out the usual junk—grocery store coupon magazines—when an envelope from the Superior Court falls out from the middle.

The judge has decided to hear my case and set a court date on the matter: 8:30 AM, May 25.

Another thirty days out.

Ugh.

Return My Son

I woke up early to bathe and dress baby Charles—who I called Charlie—nursed him, and then got myself showered.

Scanning my closet, I looked for something that could pass as business attire. Working in a call center meant the dress code was pretty casual, and the only people who ever dressed all business-like were the manager and assistant manager.

I settled on a dark pair of jeans and a blouse, telling myself it shouldn't truly matter how fancy I looked. I was going to the courthouse to right an injustice that was done to me. I was demanding that Vivian give me back my son—the one she should have never kept from me. She never adopted him and had no right to continue keeping him.

I'm an adult now.

I have every right to raise my son.

Charles was already in the car with it running when I exited the house, Charlie snug in his car seat and his diaper bag over my shoulder.

We arrived at the courthouse at 8:15 and made it through security by 8:20. I looked up at the monitor, found my name and the courtroom number, and headed in that direction.

Charlie was asleep, and I hoped he would stay that way—I was pretty sure there were rules against infants in the courtroom.

I spotted Vivian and James sitting on a bench just outside the courtroom. She had a stack of paperwork in her hand.

Beats me what for, though.

Thankfully, she didn't appear to have an attorney with her, which made me feel a little better considering I didn't hire one either.

Maybe all those papers were just an intimidation tactic.

If so, it was slightly working. I already felt underdressed for a courtroom trial, and it was clear I'd be the youngest person in the room.

I looked at the clock on the far wall.

8:29 a.m.

Just as I started to wonder how prompt the courthouse actually was, a clerk opened the courtroom doors and called both me and Vivian in.

Charles stood up at the same time I did and lifted the car seat—Charlie was still fast asleep in it. Whoever said all newborns do is eat, sleep, and shit wasn't lying.

I stepped through the courtroom doors, walking past the public observation pews and on through the low swinging doors straight to the table on the left. Two chairs had been pushed into place. I pulled out the one nearest the center of the room and sat down.

To my right was another table, where Vivian and James waddled over and seated themselves. Charles must have stayed in the back, but I didn't turn to confirm where he was seated.

I kept my head straight forward, intentionally avoiding looking at her. I hated confrontation, and it felt odd going up against her like this. I know I did nothing wrong. She was the one who lied to me. She didn't keep the promises she made. So making eye contact with her shouldn't be an issue—but it was.

"All rise for the Honorable Judge Thompson," the bailiff called out, just as a door in the back corner of the courtroom opened.

I rose, but before I was even fully standing, I heard the judge's voice: "You may be seated."

The judge was a middle-aged man with short greying hair, a round face, and thin-rimmed glasses. He had a pleasant enough look, which helped put my mind a bit at ease as anticipation built within me.

"Nicole, you are the petitioner. You have three minutes for your opening statement," the judge said.

I hadn't prepared an opening statement. I hadn't prepared any speech at all. I had felt so confident walking into this courtroom, but it was quickly dwindling.

The judge must've noticed my change in demeanor.

"Or would you like Vivian to go first?" he asked.

"Vivian can go first," I said, leaning into the small mic in the center of my table. That would give me time to think of a compelling response to whatever bullshit she was about to say.

"Good morning, Your Honor," Vivian began, her manufactured pleasant voice smooth and practiced. She had clearly mastered it over the years. "Nicole was a troubled foster child of my mother's who found herself in trouble—and pregnant."

I stared angrily at her as she spoke, her tone grating on my ears.

"She really liked my mother and didn't want to leave her placement, so she came to me for help."

I came to her, now?

Okay.

"I agreed to care for her son and adopt if need be, so that Nicole could remain in her child's life and he wouldn't end up being placed in the system or with a family Nicole didn't know. Here are the temporary guardianship papers Nicole signed shortly after giving birth." She grabbed a piece of paper from the top of her stack and stretched her arm out. The bailiff strode across the courtroom, retrieved it from Vivian, and handed it to the judge.

"It was my intention to have Nicole remain in her child's life, but she continued to get into trouble. Nicole was removed from my mother's care, and I hadn't heard from her until I got the court summons from my mother that Nicole was seeking custody."

"Do you recognize your signature on this document here?" the judge asked, prompting the bailiff to stand and walk the papers over to me.

I lifted the paper up.

It read: Temporary Guardianship.

I frowned. It wasn't an adoption paper, so I was confused as to why it was being presented as some kind of meaningful evidence.

I recognized my sloppy signature at the bottom of the two documents in front of me, still bewildered as to how this piece of paper was being used by Vanity and her attorney to prove her claim to my son—when it should have strengthened mine.

It proved I hadn't signed any adoption papers.

That she had never adopted my son.

That my child should be returned to me.

"Yes, that's my signature," I said, looking up from the documents.

"Temporary guardianship is for a period of six months or less." I listened to the judge's words, wondering where this was going. "I understand your child is three now."

I wasn't sure if he was looking for verbal confirmation or not, so I simply nodded.

"After the six-month period ended, why hadn't you gone back for your child?" the judge asked.

My mouth gaped open. He couldn't be seriously asking me this.

"I was a minor," I said. I guessed there was no way for the judge to have known my age then—or now. It wasn't like I'd been required to write my date of birth anywhere.

"I was sent away to juvenile hall, and then away to a therapeutic facility," I admitted. "I couldn't come back to get him."

The judge was silent, and I couldn't tell if this admission was helping or hurting me. I knew juvenile detention made me look like a problem, and a therapeutic group home probably didn't help either.

"Are you working?" he asked.

"Yes," I said, happy he'd finally asked a question I didn't feel like a complete idiot answering.

This was far more overwhelming and fast-paced than I had imagined it would be. My anxiety and stress levels were through the roof—I thought I might be breaking out in a cold sweat.

"Have you sent Vivian any money for the care of your son?" the judge asked.

"No."

"Anything?" the judge repeated, his voice stronger now. "Toys? Clothing? Any visits?"

Another question I had to answer no to. This was not going the way I had imagined in my head. How had Vivian managed to spin her lie about adopting my son into me abandoning him? I shook my head.

My eyes were burning with the threat of tears, and I fought not to let them fall. This was not the time to unravel.

"I made many attempts to see my son, your honor," I said. "Vivian stopped taking my calls, and shortly after that, I was sent away."

"Your Honor," Vivian spoke, interrupting in her falsely sweet voice. "Based on everything I understood about Nicole from her time in my mother's care, I believed she would take her son and potentially place him in danger. She had been making a series of poor decisions—ditching school and running away. At one point, it was thought she was on drugs."

I looked up just in time to see the judge's face change at that statement. He was starting to form a negative opinion about me, and there didn't seem to be much I could do.

"I was never on drugs, and you know that!" I spat, no longer able to keep the tears at bay.

How could this actually be happening right now?

Why was I on trial here?

"How long has the child been in your care?" the judge asked Vivian. I looked over at her and the cowardly James, who had sat next to her in silence the entire time.

"Since birth, Your Honor. I took him home from the hospital."

"And how old is the child now?"

"Three years old."

I studied the judge, waiting to see how he would respond next. He took a deep breath, as if pained.

"So for the past three years you have cared for the child's sole well-being while the plaintiff, Nicole, was in juvenile hall and treatment?"

"Yes."

"And you are wanting the child to remain in your care?"

"Yes. We would like to adopt the child, actually, and have been working with an attorney on the matter."

Another long pause from the judge.

"I understand your desire to raise your child, so it is with a heavy heart that I make this decision."

I closed my eyes and took a deep breath before opening them again. I braced myself for the bad news.

"The minor in question—albeit your son," the judge said, now speaking to me, "does not know you. You haven't seen or provided financial care for your child in three years. We are here today because you learned that at the time of birth, your child had not been adopted as you thought. You, however, had in fact wanted your child to be adopted and chose this family to adopt him."

I shook my head in utter horror, but the judge kept going.

What in the world was actually happening?

"It is my ruling that it is in the best interest of the child to stay in the care of Vivian and James. Let the record show: June 1st"—he paused to take a quick look at the clock—"8:55 a.m., Nicole Hayes's parental rights are severed on the grounds of abandonment. Court adjourned," he said, beginning to stand.

"All rise," the bailiff said.

That was it.

Just like that, it was over. I had lost my son forever to Vivian and James.

By the time I was standing, the judge had already exited the courtroom, and Vivian was packing the files she brought into her tote bag.

I pushed the courtroom door open. I couldn't even look at Charles—I was far too upset. I headed straight for the bathroom. I didn't want to get caught in the halls with Vivian or have to exit the courthouse with her behind me.

I turned on the hot water, played with the cold until it was warm, and placed my hands under it.

Warm water usually helped when I was upset, but it wasn't working this time.

I wanted to cry.

I felt more than just sadness at this unexpected defeat—this blindside.

Vivian was an entire supervillain masquerading around like Mother Theresa, and everyone just ate it up.

Deep breaths. Deep breaths.

I needed to suppress the scream building up inside of me. I couldn't let out the scream of fury fighting to escape my mouth. I was in a public bathroom. In a courthouse, at that.

I was angry and sad, and my mind just wouldn't latch on to one emotion.

I needed to grasp what in the actual hell had just happened.

Children were literally only children for eighteen years. Eighteen years. I had read a parenting pamphlet not too long ago that stated there are only 940 Saturdays from the time a child is born until they're eighteen—and that 260 of them are gone before the child is even five.

I was going to miss all 940 Saturdays with my son.

"What in the hell just happened?" I whispered out loud to myself. The process had moved so fast. I had only been in the courtroom for thirty minutes. After everything, I lost my son forever in just thirty minutes.

I knew magic wasn't real, but if it was—she would regret the day she ever deceived me. I would curse her a thousand times over. May she never find peace or happiness. Only misery.

Hot tears streamed down my face at this revelation. I guessed my mind had decided to let the grief and sorrow win out over the anger. I adjusted the cold-to-hot ratio, needing the water to be even warmer. Running my hands under warm water always seemed to do the trick when I needed to quickly rein in and regulate my emotions.

After a few minutes of this, I turned off the water and walked over to the corner wall to dry both my face and hands.

I exited the bathroom and saw Charles with baby Charlie sitting on a bench by the exit, waiting on me.

I got into the back seat of the car, completely defeated and miserable.

The judge's decision to sever my parental rights—that reality was so painful, and I didn't bear pain well.

My cognitive dissonance started to activate my critical thinking.

At Mingus Mountain, I had managed to get through the program with the sole thought of turning eighteen soon.

Eighteen—the magic number that made me an adult, enabling me to move, think, and do as I pleased. The number that finally granted you a seat at the adult table.

Yet here I was. A full-fledged adult paying taxes and other bills, but nothing had actually changed.

It was quite possible things had gotten worse.

So how did I cope now?

How did I not feel?

What did I tell myself to make not being able to see my son until he was eighteen sit right in my mind?

What lies did I need to tell myself in order to bury the grief and sense of loss I was experiencing once again?

I settled on the idea that maybe my son was better off with me having played the role of an unpaid surrogate.

Villainous Vivian was married. She provided a stable two-parent home. She had a job that actually paid her decent money, clearly. In comparison to her, what did I really have to offer my son? I had no car—he would have taken buses and cabs with me. I made $8.50 an hour and sustained myself on cereal, frozen meals, and cups of microwavable noodles. And I fell right into the statistic of being from a broken home: crackhead mother, absentee father, and little to no education since I never actually completed high school.

Maybe that was what the judge saw when he looked at my history, my clothes, and my age. Another throwaway. What I was coming to terms with now was what I already knew.

***

Maybe it was the early dinner, warm bath, and bed, but I woke with a change of heart and a renewed sense of determination.

I didn't have to be a ward-of-the-state stereotype. Just because I grew up with staff members who clocked in and out, and briefly with a self-absorbed foster mother, didn't mean I couldn't go to college and do more with my life.

I didn't have to work in a poorly run call center making $8.50 forever.

Actually, outside of money, there was no reason I couldn't go get my GED and go to college. I didn't even live that far from Glendale Community College.

Reset

I turned my car into the campus parking lot. As I approached the guard gate, I rolled down my window. A man got off his stool to greet me at my car.

"I'm here to take my GED," I said.

The guard walked back to his post and returned with a campus map. "The testing center is here," he said, pointing to the building location on the map and circling it.

"Thank you," I said, taking the map.

Opening the door to the testing center was nerve-racking. I hated tests. I felt like I knew the information well—until I was being tested on it, and then all of a sudden, my brain crashed.

Lockers lined the front side wall, a help desk sat in the front center, and rows and rows of computers filled the middle of the room. Cameras were easily visible above, angled to monitor testers.

"Here to take a test?" the woman behind the desk asked.

"Yes, the GED."

"You have your driver's license or ID?"

I reached into my purse and handed over my driver's license, watching as she typed my information into the computer before handing it back.

"You can put all your belongings in one of the lockers against the wall," she said, handing me a locker key and motioning to the wall in front of her. "No calculators allowed, but there's scratch paper at the end of each aisle, as well as a bin of pencils."

"Thanks."

Timed tests stressed me out so badly. I tried to ignore the clock counting down in the corner of the screen as I read questions and studied the answers before selecting what I believed was correct. Wondering whether I was taking too long to read through the questions—or the answers—and if I would have enough time made my stomach start to hurt.

After about five hours, I answered the last question. I considered going back through and double-checking my work. I recalled the words of a teacher I once had who said your first choice is usually the correct one and not to second-guess yourself, so I pressed the submit button and stood up.

Results were sent to the woman back at the front desk and could be printed out on the spot. As I walked back to the lockers, I told myself whatever the outcome, I wasn't going to get upset. If I had to wait a week and retest again, I would. No big deal.

"I finished testing," I said to the woman.

"Which computer number were you at?"

"58."

She typed into her computer, and I heard a paper printing.

The paper that would tell me if I passed—or needed to study harder and retake it.

I looked at the categories listed on the page with their scores and saw that I had a passing score for all five subjects—even math, which I literally passed by two points.

***

With proof that I at least had high school-level academic skills and my iden-tification card in hand, I stood in a long line behind students needing assistance with enrolling in community college. There was a stack of pamphlets on a swivel tower just on the other side of the rope next to me. I started to sift through them as I waited my turn. I had no idea what I wanted to major in—something that didn't require much math, for sure.

There were a few people working behind desks, and I tried to guess which person I'd end up getting based on my position in line. Finally next, I saw I'd be helped by a young guy who looked to be just a few years older than me.

"Hi. Looking to enroll as a student?"

"Great. I need to see a copy of your birth certificate and high school diploma or GED." I handed over the items he requested.

"Do you have a field of study in mind?"

"No, not really. Figured I would just take some prerequisite courses and decide later."

"Okay. I've gone ahead and added you into the system as a student starting the upcoming semester," he said, looking up from his computer and handing me back my items. "You're going to want to visit an academic advisor to help you select your courses and enroll in classes."

"Thanks. So how does payment work?"

"You are going to want to fill out the Free Application for Federal Student Aid. Most students qualify for a Pell Grant; however, there are other grant and scholarship programs," he said, digging into a drawer of his desk and pulling out a couple of pamphlets.

I noticed one of the pamphlets in his hand had the word foster care in the title. "Can I see that one?" I asked, pointing at it.

"Of course." He handed me the brochure and I read the title: Foster Care to Success Education and Training Voucher.

Opening up the pamphlet, I quickly read through the program:

The Education and Training Voucher (ETV) is an annual federal grant provided to states to fund youth who have aged out of the foster care system and who are enrolled in college, university, and vocational training programs.

Youth must be in foster care, adopted from foster care after age 16, or aged out of foster care.

Provides up to $20,000 over the course of a college career or training program.

Arizona ETV recipients must maintain a minimum 2.5 GPA each term. Students must submit an academic transcript showing grades and GPA from the most recently completed semester/term.

$5,000 a semester. I quickly did the easy math in my head. Well, if that wasn't incentive enough to get an education…

"Wow," I finally said after the shock wore off. "I was a ward of the state and in foster care and I never knew this program existed."

"Well, keep the flier," he said with a smile. "Just get everything filled out and turned in as soon as possible so there won't be any delays in financial aid or your start date."

"Thanks," I said, getting up from his desk and looking at the long line of students waiting to see an academic advisor. "I just stand in that line now?" I asked.

"Yes," he said, already looking at his computer to call the next student in line.

***

I sat in the front row with my notebook open and a brand new sharpened pencil ready to take notes. I had made sure to get the textbooks for all my classes in advance—a backpack, laptop, and pencils—so that I would be fully prepared for my first day of school. I looked around at the other students in the classroom. They all seemed to be prepared too, with their laptops and notebooks out on the tables in front of them.

As the teacher spoke about the syllabus and what we were going to be covering over the course of the semester, I started to get worried. I had barely passed my GED, and that knowledge was a bit intimidating.

Honestly, I didn't even know how I managed it. I had attended high school for such a short period of time, and when I had been there, I was distracted with pregnancy.

I sort of felt like an imposter sitting in class. I imagined most of these kids had actually finished all four years of high school. They were probably only attending a community college to save on money—and not because they were high school dropouts like myself.

Between the Pell Grant and the foster care scholarship I received, school was covered as long as my grades stayed a C+ or higher. While I didn't think of myself as stupid or anything, I definitely felt like I was missing vital information—things I might have learned had I not gotten pregnant and dropped out.

My nervousness stemmed from the feeling of being behind. I had an incomplete 10th-grade education, and I was now attending college classes.

Despite the rough start, I managed to complete my degree—a bachelor's in Communications—and not a moment too soon.

So Much Has Happened

Like a damn fool, I had still been holding out hope Charles would officially choose me. We weren't together together, but he would still come over to my apartment and even watch Charlie if I really needed him to. We both had our own place in the same apartment complex, so it was easy to get fooled.

I saw the light when he came into some money. I didn't know how or even why he suddenly had extra cash—all I knew was what he did with it. He gave some to his ex-wife. Yeah, the same ex-wife who had divorced him for having had a relationship and child with me. But what really fucked me up was him announcing that he had purchased a motorcycle.

Nothing for his baby momma. Granted, he was only kind of claiming our son at this point.

But his ex-wife had a car to transport their child in, he had a car—a convertible, actually—and me? I walked and took the bus, carrying a heavy-ass car seat on my arm. And he went out and purchased a motorcycle.

Things got messy. I made it clear he wasn't even to climb the steps to my apartment. I didn't want to see him, let alone breathe the same air. Our on-again, off-again situationship—that I had honestly thought was love—was over.

When my lease was up, I moved out of the apartment complex I shared with Charles and tried supporting myself the best way I knew how. All of this pissed Charles off so much that he switched up and started acting like father of the year. He took me to court demanding custody of the child he, only weeks ago, had no real interest in providing for.

Charles took me to court not once, not twice, but four times.

The first time, the judge gave him and me 50/50 custody, and that's how it was for about a year. Then we went back again. And again. Each year, until Charles was finally granted full custody.

He did something even I didn't see coming. He waltzed into the courtroom with images of me that he had printed out. The images depicted me in seductive lingerie advertising escort services.

Like wow, this is what we were doing now?

Charles stood in front of the judge with a straight face and said he was concerned that any one of my clients might become disgruntled and return when our son was in my care. So he was concerned about his safety.

All this from the man who would literally sneak into one of my foster mother's sliding back doors while she slept to sleep with me and hand me money. The same man who parked around corners while I was living at group homes, waiting for me to come join him in the car.

Basically, it was completely safe when he did it—but dangerous if anyone else might.

I didn't bother mentioning all of this to the judge. It just seemed like it would make me appear like even more of a lowlife.

With photo proof of his claims and a mask of genuine concern, there was nothing I could really say other than "okay" when the judge awarded Charles full custody and me visitation at Charles's discretion.

Having won and needing me to beg to see my son wasn't enough punishment, though. At the end of the school year, Charlie had his birthday party—which was completely awkward with us all in attendance—but after the party, Charles told me they were moving when the school year was up.

Knowing there was nothing I could do to prevent the move, I spiraled hard. Like, partying every day just to avoid being home in an empty house. Drinking all the time to the point of getting a DUI. Losing my job at Amazon. And the icing on the cake? Getting evicted.

I was also officially charged with advertising as an escort without a license. I racked up a few more charges because, at that point, why not? The only thing making me different from my sister and biological parents at that point was drugs. I had set out to try and better my life and obtain an education, but all I managed to do was affirm the stereotype.

Can't fight DNA.

Not wanting to be homeless and living on the streets like I had chosen to do as a teenager, I decided I would go to an ex-client of mine's home. No more boxcar kids—that shit was a dangerous game. Matt and I weren't exactly friends anymore, but we had been friendly at one point. That all changed when he punched me in the face, though, and I hadn't spoken to him since. This could turn out to be another poor decision, but I didn't have too many options. Him or the streets, really.

I waited until it was evening and then called a cab I wouldn't be able to pay for if he didn't let me in.

It was dark by the time I arrived at his doorstep, and I knocked a few times.

"Hey," I said as casually as possible when he opened the door.

"Nicole?" He looked at me, confused.

"Yeah. Can I come in?"

He stepped forward out of the doorway, eyeing the cab parked in front of his house.

"Also, I don't have money for the car."

He wanted to say no—I could see it in his body language.

"I don't have anywhere else to go."

That got him moving. He went to pay the cab, and I walked in and sat on the couch for a bit. It was extra awkward, and I really didn't know what to say.

After a couple of nights on the living room sofa, he told me I could just sleep in his office. I didn't know how long I did this, but long enough to get through Devious Maids, Desperate Housewives, and several seasons of Army Wives before he told me I needed to find a job and leave. That he had a girlfriend now and wanted her to start coming over—and didn't want her to meet me.

I went on Craigslist and started applying to jobs. None of the jobs I applied to bothered responding.

"Just find a volunteer position," Matt said, clearly annoyed by my lack of progress. "Those typically turn into full-time paid positions."

I saw a post for the Blind Veterans Association and decided to apply. I explained in my email that I had previously volunteered at the American Cancer Society and was experienced in cold calling and fundraising. I got an almost immediate response and was asked to meet the following morning.

After two bus rides, I arrived in a residential neighborhood in the heart of central Phoenix. I quickly learned the Blind Veterans Association had one member. He was an 85-year-old Korean War vet looking for a personal assistant and chauffeur.

It was a plot twist, but I had nothing better to do with my time outside of watching Netflix in Matt's office or lounging by his pool. The lounging by the pool wasn't so bad—except for the fact that he didn't want me there at all.

I took Jerome, the not-so-blind vet, to the casino almost every evening and sat with him as he played hand after hand of poker. During the day, I drove him around in his car to run errands.

After a few weeks of this, his grandson stopped by the house to both check on him and see who the lady helping his grandfather was. Once I met Jerome's grandson—whose name I learned was Mendel—we were inseparable.

Our first date was a double date with his grandfather at the kosher pizza store, then the casino, and the next thing I knew, I was moving in and studying to convert to Judaism.

After five years of knowing Mendel and two years of studying everything I needed to know, I had finished all my classes and would be dipping in the mikvah in the morning and having a wedding that evening. With just two and a half months until the conversion and wedding, I had a lot to plan.

I was finally about to become a part of a family—his. I hadn't met all of his family yet, but I knew I would be meeting most of them on my wedding day.

Engagement

I walked into the bridal shop with absolutely no idea what kind of dress I wanted. The funny thing was I loved watching the show Bridezillas and knew the dress was important—that I was supposed to just know the right dress once I tried it on—but the store was literally filled with rows of dresses taking up the front all the way to the back.

The right side of the store had a stage of sorts and a massive mirror that stretched across the entire stage, with three small changing rooms off to the side. It was a lot to take in.

"Do you have any idea what style of dress you might like?" a very enthusiastic young woman asked. When I didn't immediately reply, she continued, "Maybe a price range to start in?"

I hadn't thought about how much we were gonna spend, but anything over a thousand was out of the question for sure.

The woman grabbed three of the most popular styles in my size and handed them to me. I followed her to the changing room and let her help me into them.

Looking in the mirror, I couldn't decide if I actually liked any of the dresses—and then my phone began to buzz.

I swiped the green icon on my phone and placed it to my ear.

"Hey babe," I said.

"Where are you?" Mendel asked.

"Trying on dresses at the bridal store near the mall," I told him.

"I'm not far," he said. "I'll meet you there."

I was back in my clothes when Mendel arrived.

"Let me see the dresses you picked out."

"Well, I wasn't really crazy about any of the dresses," I said. "I was going to have another look around."

"Stay here, I'll find you a dress," he said and disappeared.

When he returned, he had one dress in his hand. I tried it on—this time actually leaving the dressing room and stepping onto the platform, facing myself in the mirror.

"That's the one," he said.

"Yeah, that really looks nice on you," an older man I hadn't noticed before said. Probably the father of a soon-to-be bride.

I knew people often see you differently than how you see yourself, so I figured if my soon-to-be husband thought this was the dress, along with this random man, then this must, in fact, be the dress. We checked out and placed the dress in the trunk of my car.

Leaning against the trunk, I reached my arms out and wrapped them around Mendel's waist.

"Calls have slowed down, it seems. Do you want to go and grab a suit?" I asked.

With Mendel being an on-call mobile locksmith, I never really knew when he'd be busy running around the city or when he'd have free time, so I figured I should make the most of whatever time we had before he got busy again.

"Yeah, sure," he said, hugging me back and giving me a kiss on the forehead.

"It's off Camelback," I said, looking into his big brown eyes. "Probably fifteen minutes away."

"Okay, I'll meet you there. Hopefully I won't get a job."

"You know if you do, you can always say you aren't available and pass it to an independent contractor."

I knew he wouldn't actually do that, but I said it anyway. Whenever I wanted him to fully focus on me and not split his time between me and work, I said this. He was a workaholic though, and could never turn down a job if he didn't absolutely have to.

The suit and tuxedo store was just as busy and overwhelming as the bridal shop. The entire outer wall was lined with dress shirts, suit jackets, and tuxedos. The middle of the room had a platform similar to the bridal store, with mirrors so the person standing there could get a good look at themselves in whatever they were trying on.

We wandered around the store a bit, watching other shoppers being helped, trying on suit pants and dress shirts, before a woman approached us and asked if she could help.

"We're just looking for a nice suit. We're getting married at the end of February," I said.

"Congratulations!" she said with a well-practiced smile. I bet her mouth hurt at the end of the day. "Just two months away!"

I smiled and nodded.

The woman brought Mendel to the back and began to take his measurements.

"Is Charlie going to be coming? Should we get him a suit too?"

"No. Spring break isn't happening until three weeks after, sadly. So he'll barely miss it."

"Probably better that way."

"Why?" I asked, curious as to why he wouldn't just have a neutral stance. The wedding happening before Charlie's spring break wasn't done intentionally. The end of February was just the soonest the venue we had chosen would be available next. And honestly, weddings couldn't be that exciting for a child—especially a religious one that was going to follow strict customs and rituals.

"So the thought is that children of the bride or groom might experience emotional turmoil and conflict when a parent remarries. Since the wedding is meant to be a joyous occasion for all, having a child that might have been holding out hope his or her mother and father might get back together would not be happy. At least, that is the Chabad custom."

"I see, I see," I said, nodding my head as I continued to watch the woman get Mendel's measurements. "Well, you know me and Charlie's dad were never married."

Actually, I was sure Charlie didn't remember a time when me and his dad were together. He was two years old when we split up, and I'm pretty sure memories don't stick that early.

Charlie was six years old, about to turn seven, when he came on a plane for his first spring break and met Mendel—and he really liked him. So I highly doubted he would have an issue with us being married. Mendel took Charlie on jobs with him when I had to work, built Legos with him, and played video games, so they were pretty much good pals.

I could only think of one time Charlie even asked about me and his father. I had been spending the week in Texas for his birthday and had stayed in a hotel. He asked why I didn't live with him and his dad, and I just told him me and his father didn't get along. He seemed to accept that answer because he didn't ask any sort of follow-up questions like "Why not?"

"All the bridesmaids will be wearing gold, so it would be nice if we can find him a gold tie." I pulled my phone out of my purse and showed the woman a picture of the dress my bridesmaids—which were all five of Mendel's sisters— would be wearing.

After a while of searching, I found what I believed to be the perfect color match for the bridesmaids' dresses: a solid, coppery-gold piece of fabric that I never would have imagined cost $58.

Next was choosing the dress shirt, which I wanted to make sure matched the long white Kittel he would be wearing during the wedding ceremony. There were so many different shades of white that even this took some time, but so far Mendel's phone hadn't rung, so we had time.

When we were finally ready to check out after trying on a myriad of pant sizes, the store was ready to close. I learned that one dress pant brand's 32-inch waist didn't mean the next brand's 32-inch waist would fit, and we had to play around with sizes.

All the shopping and standing up walking around large stores had me exhausted and ready to go relax.

With the venue decided and all major purchases taken care of, that left me to find small mementos that would complete our themes and make for a great time. Basically, we were just waiting for the big day to arrive.

Alert

I was an hour into my hair appointment at Caribbean Hair Braiding. I had been going there for years and loved how quickly they could do my hair. I was still two months away from my wedding and knew I'd have to do this all over again the week before so I could have a fresh retwist.

Two hours passed, and they were more than halfway done with my head, but I was beginning to feel antsy and restless in my seat. Sitting still had never been easy for me.

Two women, speaking in strong accents to each other, were on either side of my head, tugging as if I were the rope in a tug-of-war. Simply listening to music was no longer enough to distract me from the tight pulling and pain, so I opened up my social media app. Almost immediately, I noticed I had received a couple of likes and had a message waiting for me.

One new message in bold font stared at me, waiting for me to click on it.

Hey, was all it said.

I stared at the tiny circle with the male figure in it. It was such a small picture, but I knew I had never received a message from this person before.

All I could make out was that the figure looked pretty young—well, younger than me—and that he'd had a recent haircut because the lines outlining his hair looked fresh.

The thought of deleting the message crossed my mind. Messages on this app from people you don't know are usually from someone in another country trying to scam you, but with at least two more hours in this chair, I figured, Why not entertain whatever the scam might be? I could always press the block button later.

I clicked on the small circle to enlarge the image and see the full figure. I leaned my head down in disbelief to stare closer at it, only to have my head immediately jerked back up by the woman on my right.

It was my son.

I had a message from my son that just said, Hey.

I knew it was him the second the image enlarged. In true stalker fashion, I had been visiting Vanity's social media page, hoping to spot him in her photos. I would have checked Vivian's page too, but hers was private, and I had no intention of sending her a friend request.

Most of Vanity's posts were just pictures of herself dressed up, pictures of food she was about to eat, or memes. But the last time I visited her page, I saw him. He was standing next to Vanity and Vivian in a marching band uniform, in what looked like a school parking lot.

A surge of excitement rushed through me—the kind of feeling you get when you're about to ride a roller coaster.

This was crazy. This was the kind of thing that happened in movies, not in real life.

After that horrible day at the courthouse, when I tried and failed to get my son back from Vivian, I was certain I wouldn't see or speak to him again until he turned 18 years old. I'd planned to track him down when that day came, to explain who I was, but now here he was, on the internet, reaching out to me.

This… this was some Finding Carter type of thing.

I reined in my emotions, not wanting to upset the two women still aggressively tugging at my hair.

Me: Hello. How's life?

The response came immediately.

Jayshawn: Wait. You know who I am?

Life is coo. Hbu?

Me: Yeah, why wouldn't I?

Good. Getting my hair twisted.

I didn't mention that I had initially assumed he was just a random scammer or creep. Once I saw his photo and username, I knew exactly who he was.

Jayshawn: Cause I look different. I got my hair done a week ago but I took it out.

Me: You don't look different. Just older. So you don't leave your hair in long, huh?

If anything, I'm shocked you knew who I was.

Jayshawn: I didn't until recently.

Me: Oh, okay. Who told you?

Jayshawn: I found out myself.

Me: Oh yeah? Clever kid. So how'd you figure it out?

Jayshawn: I was going to get my nose pierced, and I had to go through paperwork. I was putting two and two together and found out.

Me: Like a birth certificate?

Jayshawn: Nah, these court documents. The birth certificate don't really say nothing except my birthday.

Me: I see.

Of course, his birth certificate wouldn't say anything. It would list his adoptive parents' names. A complete forgery, in my opinion—state-issued lies. It was crazy to me how a birth certificate could just be rewritten to erase a child's biological identity and connections.

I always knew I was adopted. I couldn't see why it was such a big secret for some families. I could only imagine how many people have lived their entire lives unaware, only to find out after their "parents" passed away or during a medical emergency that they had been adopted. It was cruel.

Me: So did you get your nose pierced?

Jayshawn: No.

Me: Oh, haha.

Jayshawn: It didn't happen cause I started talking to my aunt about being adopted and stuff.

Me: Aunt? Tashia?

Tashia was one of Vanity's four daughters. She had lived in the same house as me but on the opposite side of the split-floor plan. Her room was in the front near the living room, while mine was in the back near Vanity's. She had already graduated high school and was practically an adult when we lived together, so I barely saw her. She was either in her room or out with friends for days at a time. When we did interact, it was always pleasant enough, but we never made much effort to bond.

Jayshawn: Yeah.

Me: I see. So what did she say?

I wanted to know exactly what kind of lies had been fed to him about me. Technically, Tashia wasn't the liar here—unless she'd repeated whatever bull Vivian had told him.

Jayshawn: Nothing really. She had me talk to my mom.

My chest tightened at the word mom. It felt like a stab to the heart, but I kept my response measured.

Me: Aww. So you're okay with this information?

Jayshawn: Yeah, I'm not trippin' or nothing. It was just shocking.

Me: I feel that.

No kidding, it was shocking. He had no idea he was adopted. He had no idea I even existed until recently. What assholes they were for keeping this from him. If he hadn't found the paperwork, he might never have known. Well—not until I tracked him down and told him.

Jayshawn: How old is Charlie?

I smiled at his question, happy that he wanted to know about his half-brother. I also appreciated that he was keeping the conversation light.

Me: He's 11.

Jayshawn: He in Texas?

Me: Yeah. He moved to Texas a few years ago now, but he comes to Phoenix often.

Jayshawn: Oh, that's wassup. I heard he likes Fortnite!

Me: Yep. Who told you that?

Jayshawn: Social media.

I laughed, realizing what he meant. Not too long ago, I'd posted a picture of Charlie at a Walmart Supercenter. He'd found a floppy leather hat and a plastic pickaxe, pretending to chop at things. I snapped a few photos and uploaded them with the caption:

Getting some supplies… building his defenses #reallifefortnite.

Me: That's awesome. Haha. No secrets on the internet.

Jayshawn: I'm good at Fortnite, but I don't play that much cause I don't have a PlayStation. Whenever I go to my friend's, I'll play.

Me: You don't have a Switch either?

What teenager didn't have some sort of gaming device? That seemed crazy to me.

Me: Charlie plays on the Switch, but you can also play on a PC.

Jayshawn: Don't have none of that.

That hit hard. Charlie had so much compared to him, and it was clear that Jayshawn knew it. He had obviously been on my social media before reaching out to me, and he'd seen everything—photos of Charlie, photos of me, and likely a decade's worth of posts showcasing the life I'd built.

Jayshawn: How old are you?

Thank goodness he changed the subject. I was already struggling to hold back my opinions about Vivian so I wouldn't come across as toxic or bitter. I didn't want Jayshawn to feel like his life would've been better off without me.

Me: 30. December 22, I'll be 31.

Jayshawn: How old do you think I am?

He was testing me.

Me: 16.

Jayshawn: Close. I'm 15.

Me: Aww.

Jayshawn: Anything else you want to know about me?

Another test.

Me: Well, I know you're in a band. You and Charlie have that in common, actually. He plays the trombone. What do you play?

Instead of asking a question, I shared something I already knew about him. I wanted him to know that I had been keeping tabs on him the best I could. I wanted him to know that, while I'd had to put him out of my mind to move on with my life, I'd never truly forgotten him. I still loved him and wished I had been the one to raise him.

Jayshawn: Well, I'm no longer in marching band, but I played percussion instruments. I'm really good. I'll prolly play next year.

Me: That's nice. #drumline

I had been playing it cool so far, keeping everything surface-level. I had imagined meeting him many times, but I had never really considered what I would say or how the conversation might go. I didn't want to come across as over-eager, pushy, or even creepy.

He was a minor. My son, yes, but still a minor. I hesitated before typing:

We should meet, if you'd like that.

I stared at the message before deleting it.

Minutes passed, and I felt I needed to say something. He'd reached out to me for a reason.

Me: Well, do you want to meet?

I pressed send and quickly turned my phone over. If he said no, I would be gutted. I counted to 60 before flipping the phone back over.

Jayshawn: Say less.

Me: Does your mother care that you're speaking to me?

"Mother." I hated that I had to use that word to refer to Vivian. He had known her as his mother all his life, and I didn't want to push him away by showing my bitterness.

Jayshawn: I'm not finna tell.

His use of the word mother felt like another stab to the heart, but I played it cool.

He didn't need to know how I felt. He hadn't asked me any questions about how everything played out or how he came to be adopted, so I wasn't going to bring it up either. I also didn't care that he had no intention of telling Vivian he'd found me.

Screw her.

I shouldn't have had to wait this long to connect with my son in the first place. The fact that he'd reached out to me on his own, something Vivian couldn't stop or control, gave me an immense sense of joy.

Because screw her and all her lies and fake kindness.

Jayshawn: Where do you live?

Me: Off 12th Street and Northern in Phoenix.

Jayshawn: Oh, okay.

Me: Are you still in Mesa?

Jayshawn: Yep. But we should link.

A burst of excitement pulsed through me. He was serious about wanting to meet me.

I typed, I'm having a birthday party at an arcade on the 15th, and attached my phone number. I figured offering a public place to meet would make things less awkward or intimidating.

Jayshawn: Well, I'll see, but I wanna meet you in private. And bring my friend with me.

Me: Okay. Well, let me know. I'm around.

Jayshawn: But where?

Seeing that he didn't want to meet at an arcade, I sent him my home address and asked if he needed a ride.

Jayshawn: Nope, but we should go to the mall.

Me: Okay. What mall?

Jayshawn: Up to you.

This kid hadn't liked any of my suggestions so far, and I didn't want to keep throwing out the wrong ideas. I didn't care where we met as long as we did.

Me: What mall is near you?

Jayshawn: Fashion Square. I've never been there, but I've heard a lot about it.

Me: Okay, we can meet there.

Jayshawn: Okay, say less. But I'm bringing my friend and probably my godbrother.

Me: Okay, fine. When?

Jayshawn: Idk.

Me: Okay.

Jayshawn: I gotta see when I have a ride.

Me: Okay. I gotta put my phone on the charger.

Jayshawn: It's all good. I gotta go anyways.

Not Waiting

I opened my eyes the next morning and instinctively felt around for my phone. Normally, I would check my emails first, but today I went straight to the social media app. A green dot near my son's username let me know he was online.

Me: Hey, what are your plans for today? Did you want to try and meet up today?

Jayshawn: My mom said we should invite you over to my grandmother's for Christmas. All the family goes to her place for holiday get-togethers.

So much for not telling Vivian he'd reached out to me. Clearly, this kid—my son—couldn't actually keep a secret.

I wondered what could have happened in the ten hours since I'd last spoken to him. We had gone from secretly meeting at a mall with his friend to waiting until Christmas to meet—surrounded by his "mom," my former foster mother, and a host of people I wanted nothing to do with.

I had absolutely no desire for my first meeting with my son—who I hadn't seen since he was a baby—to be overshadowed by Vivian or Vanity. They'd both act like saviors instead of the liars and manipulators they truly were, and the whole thing would be painfully awkward.

When I first asked Jayshawn if he planned on telling Vivian he'd found me, I was open to any answer. But once he said he wasn't going to tell her, I preferred it that way. Now, here we were—with her not only knowing, but inviting me to a family holiday gathering as if we were some picture-perfect group.

I hadn't even told my fiancé about any of this yet. Last night, I'd come home so late, my head hurting from all the tugging at the braiding salon, that I just took some Tylenol and went straight to bed.

With Christmas apparently being the new timeline, I decided to make small talk and get to know him a little better in the meantime.

Me: So, what do you normally do on the weekends?

Jayshawn: I like playing Fortnite, but I can only do that if I'm at my friend's house.

Right. He had mentioned yesterday that he didn't have a gaming system. I still couldn't believe it. What teenager didn't have a gaming device of some kind? He didn't even have a desktop or laptop computer. How did he turn in homework assignments?

I grew up in shelters, group homes, foster care, and even a treatment center, and every single one had some kind of gaming system. In the group home, we'd play card games like Speed, Slapjack, and Uno—which could get crazy intense. There was also a shared computer we took turns using to play Tetris or Minesweeper. We even had a Sega Genesis to play Sonic. I couldn't believe Vivian—this woman who had fought tooth and nail to adopt him—couldn't provide him with something so basic.

Even homeless people had cell phones these days.

Me: So you need your own PlayStation to play with your friends?

Jayshawn: Basically.

Me: Do you want me to head over to your side of town? It would only take me 30 minutes. I could bring you a PlayStation.

Jayshawn: You would do that?

Yes. Yes, I would. I had no intention of waiting until Christmas—a holiday I didn't even celebrate—to meet my son for the first time, especially not while surrounded by people I despised. If the price of meeting him alone was a $499 PlayStation, then so be it.

Me: Absolutely. I'm free right now.

Jayshawn: And you're going to bring me a PlayStation?

Me: Yes. I can pick one up now.

Jayshawn: Look up Windmill Apartments in Mesa. That's where I am right now. It's an apartment complex next to my house. I'm sitting in the gym.

I quickly googled the location he gave me. It was only 25 minutes away. I expected as much since I lived in Phoenix and he lived in Mesa. A 25-minute drive was nothing. To reassure him, I sent a screenshot of the route.

Me: I'll need to make a stop at Best Buy, so give me 45 minutes total.

Jayshawn: That gives me time to get dressed.

Recalling how plans had suddenly shifted last night—from secretly meeting at the mall to waiting until Christmas—I needed to make sure he wouldn't back out on me again.

Me: Okay, don't have me drive all the way out there, and you're not there.

Jayshawn: I'm gonna be there, haha. I'm not a flake, but you can't tell anyone we met.

Me: Don't tell?

Jayshawn: Yeah, 'cause they don't want me meeting you until Christmas. If they found out I saw you…

It wasn't like I planned to call Vivian and announce anything. I didn't even have her number. I had zero desire to see or deal with her. I just hoped Jayshawn wouldn't mention anything to her in the time it took me to grab the PlayStation and drive to him.

I jumped out of bed and quickly threw on a sweater dress and fuzzy slippers before heading to the living room. My fiancé was sitting on the couch in a T-shirt and sweatpants, a coffee cup in one hand and his phone in the other, likely reading the news.

While I'd rather not have had to explain this situation to him, I knew leaving the house on a Sunday with no explanation would look sketchy.

"Hey, so do you remember how I told you I got pregnant in high school and had a son?" I asked casually, already at the front door with my keys in hand.

"Yeah, why?" he said, not even looking up from his phone.

"Well, he messaged me a couple of days ago and wants to meet," I said, still trying to sound nonchalant.

"You're going to meet him now? Is that a good idea?" he asked, finally looking up.

"I mean, I already told him I'd be there in 45 minutes, so…"

Good idea or bad idea, I was going. I didn't bother mentioning that I'd secured this meeting by offering to buy my son a PlayStation.

"Well, are you going to tell him what an asshole Vivian is and how she basically kidnapped him?"

"No. Why in the world would I say that to him?"

"So he knows what a monster the woman he calls mother is."

"No," I said firmly. "I'm just going to meet him, hear what he has to say, answer any questions, and leave all that drama out of it." I reached for the door. "I'll let you know how it goes."

Meeting my Son

Pulling into the apartment complex, I wasn't entirely sure where to park. I chose one spot, but after five minutes, I started questioning whether I'd be able to see him walking up. I also realized I hadn't told him which car I'd be in. Backing out of the spot, I looked for a more visible area where someone walking could easily see who was in the car, and I could have a clear view both behind and in front of me.

Another five minutes passed, and I decided it would be better to get out of the car altogether. I walked over to a sitting area just outside the gym near the pool.

Finally, I saw him—a tall, lean boy approaching in black pants that barely fit him, sagging past his waist, and a white T-shirt that ended just at the top of the pants.

This is him.

Holy shit.

Okay, calm down. Act like a calm, cool, and collected individual.

I wondered if he cared for hugs. Should I hug him? I personally didn't like hugs, and maybe he wasn't the hugging type either. He didn't know me.

Forgetting the hug, I quickly handed him the Best Buy bag with the PlayStation in it. "Here," I said, taking a seat. He sat down in the chair next to mine.

Silence hung in the air. We were both waiting for the other to break the ice and start the conversation.

"Who are you going to say bought you a PlayStation if you don't want your mother to know we met?" I asked finally.

"I'll just say it's old and that my best friend TJ let me have his."

I'd learned from Jayshawn that TJ was one of nine children and that they'd been friends since he was 10 years old.

"Solid enough plan," I said. "Always stay as close to the truth as possible when telling a lie you don't want to get caught in." I smiled.

"You grew up with my grandmother? She was your foster mom?"

"Yes. I only stayed with her for a couple of years, though."

"How did you like living with her?"

"She wasn't bad, I guess. Spent a lot of time chasing after a married man named Stanley."

"No way. I remember him! He was married?"

"Yeah. Some days she'd take me with her to his shop to spend time with him in secret. I'd be sitting in the car for hours, hungry, just waiting for her."

"That's crazy. He still has the junkyard or whatever it was—all those broken-down cars."

I let out a laugh. "So, how do you like Vanity?" I didn't really feel like calling her his grandmother. She wasn't.

"I feel like I was the only grandkid she spanked."

"What? Why would she spank you?"

Vanity never spanked me. She never even yelled at me. I was a ward of the state, so maybe that had something to do with it, but she'd never struck me as angry or violent.

"Said I talked back and was disrespectful."

This news upset me a lot. The fact that she had hit him at all was crazy, but the fact that she only hit him? That was infuriating.

"She was always putting me to work, you know? Having me do chores all day or running useless errands with her."

So, outside of picking up a habit of hitting small children, she hadn't changed much—still needy and self-absorbed.

Jayshawn shared how Vivian was pretty strict and that he mostly just went to school and came home. Sometimes, when she was gone and he was bored or hungry, he'd walk to his Aunt Tashia's house, which wasn't far. Tashia had internet and paid TV subscriptions, making her house a preferred option when TJ's wasn't available. He admitted that Vivian didn't give him any spending money, so he often resorted to stealing things like clothing or food. He also mentioned he usually rode the light rail without paying.

"Does she not have a job?" I asked, trying to understand how she could be struggling so much to provide for one child.

"Yeah, some insurance firm."

"Oh, cool," I said, pretending to care. "Like a call center? Or what does she do?"

"I don't really know, for real."

"How much does she make?" I finally just flat-out asked.

"Shi, I don't know that either, but she works long hours, sometimes getting home around 8 p.m."

I let the matter go and shifted the conversation to James, whom I hadn't heard about yet.

"Where's your father?" I asked, wanting to use the title he was familiar with.

"Kansas."

"What? Really?"

Apparently, not long after the adoption, James divorced Vivian and moved to Kansas. He didn't pay child support or help Vivian in any way. Jayshawn had lived with James for about a year but eventually returned to Arizona because he didn't get along with James's new girlfriend.

"No way," I said, unable to hide my surprise. I had been trying to stay neutral during our chats, but this was unexpected. "When did he leave? When did you go to Kansas?"

"I was probably about four when he left. And let me think," he paused. "I must've been nine since I met TJ when I was 10."

After coming back from Kansas, Jayshawn spent the summer with Vanity in West Phoenix. He met TJ that summer while shooting hoops in Vanity's driveway. When his basketball bounced into TJ's yard, Jayshawn ran after it, tripped, and fell. TJ saw and came to check if he was okay. They had been best friends ever since, and Jayshawn even called TJ's mom "Mom."

Hearing this hurt. Vivian hadn't given Jayshawn the love he needed. She hadn't been nurturing, and he was forced to create a pseudo-family. I didn't know who Destiny was, but I was grateful she had shown my son love and kindness when I couldn't—and when Vivian hadn't.

"Destiny was the first person I told," he said.

"Really?" I asked, feeling a twinge of jealousy at the fact that a woman I had never met was the person he turned to for important things. It was an irrational thought—I had just met him—but I wanted to be the person he turned to, as his mother.

"I was in shock," he said. "I grabbed my phone, snapped a photo of the paperwork, and came over here to the gym to call Destiny."

I thought about how I hadn't immediately told anybody once I realized it was my son who had messaged me on social media. I was too busy being excited and getting to know him. It wasn't until the next day that I told my fiancé. On the drive up, I had quickly called two of my close friends, telling them I would explain how the meeting went afterward.

"What did she say?" I asked.

"She didn't believe me. She was shocked too."

I could see why people might be shocked—Vivian and Jayshawn shared the same deep Mahogany skin complexion. But what I noticed right away was that we shared familial facial expressions and mannerisms.

After he spoke with Destiny and got over his initial shock, he walked over to Tashia's house to ask her about me. She shared with him my social media pages, which I hadn't bothered to make private, and that was how—and when—he messaged me the simple "hey."

We spent the next 20 minutes making small talk and laughing about the things we had in common. I asked if he had any questions about his birth or adoption, but he said no. I was relieved. Although I had anticipated tough questions, I was glad I didn't have to answer them yet. The entire situation was uncharted territory, and I hated being overly emotional around people. I would much rather sit in a room or car alone and unpack my feelings while listening to sad music than risk having a full-on breakdown in front of people.

Jayshawn seemed to want to keep the conversation surface-level, and that was okay with me.

Eventually, I became uncomfortable sitting in the open area. The heat was unbearable, and I was thirsty and hungry. Despite having lived in Arizona most of my life, I never carried water like most locals did. I also began to wonder if Vivian ever came to this complex looking for him. Did she even know he came here to use the internet?

"Do you want to grab a bite to eat?" I finally asked.

"Yeah," he said eagerly, and I got the feeling he was the type of kid who was always ready to eat.

"It's the yellow Jeep right there," I said, pointing to my car. He followed me to it and climbed into the passenger seat.

As I pulled out of the complex, I briefly questioned my actions. Meeting him in secret was one thing, but picking him up and taking him somewhere? I pushed the thought away. He was already in the car, and he was my son, after all. I should not need permission to spend time with him.

We found a Chinese restaurant, and lunch went well. I was glad he felt comfortable enough with me to talk and didn't insist on involving—ahem— his "mother." Afterward, I dropped him off at the same complex just behind his and headed home.

I had so much to tell my fiancé and friends about our meeting and how it went.

Silent Night

I was starting to quickly understand that there wasn't much Jayshawn did without a friend—and typically, that friend was TJ. I also noticed that he told TJ's mother, Destiny, everything. The only reason I was able to meet him alone at all was because of the last-minute nature of it, coupled with the fact that he really wanted the PlayStation 4. I knew that and used it to my advantage. I didn't want a bunch of onlookers at our first meeting or for it to turn into a Maury episode.

My GPS directed me to a house with a gravel front yard, toys scattered about, cigarette butts littering the ground, and old, forgotten muscle cars parked to the side. It was typical of a home in West Phoenix and reminded me of the neighborhood I lived in with Vanity as a teen. Many of the yards in that area, while large, were unkempt. People with limited incomes didn't bother spending money or time on maintaining grass, replacing rocks, or trimming bushes and trees when they had bills they could barely pay.

I watched as a tall, skinny white woman with long, thick blonde hair walked out of the house, cradling a baby in one arm and holding a cigarette in the other.

So this is Destiny.

Trailing behind her was a pack of small children. One of them let out a string of curse words as the apparent tail end of an argument spilled out. I was shocked to hear such colorful language from someone so little.

I hadn't planned on getting out of the car, so I rolled down my window.

"Hey," I said, glancing past her, looking for Jayshawn. But he hadn't come outside with her.

"So, you're Jayshawn's birth mother?" she asked, taking a drag of her cigarette. "I had my son TJ at 16 too." She was trying to be relatable, but unless she was also a ward of the state, I knew our circumstances couldn't have been the same.

"Oh."

"I can't believe you really bought him a PlayStation 4. When he told me, I was like, 'There's no way she's just going to buy you a PlayStation; she's trying to impress you.' But then he called me after you guys went out to eat and said you really showed up with a PlayStation." She recited the play-by-play of my meeting with Jayshawn, and I just stared at her.

This kid holds nothing back from her, I see. I guess it's good he has someone he trusts completely.

"Are you, like, rich or something?" she asked, but didn't give me time to answer before she started talking again. "You know he needs a cellphone. The one he has is one of the girls' old phones, and it doesn't have any service."

"Yeah, he mentioned he needed a phone," I said, reaching over to the passenger-side floor to grab my old cellphone. "I went to the T-Mobile store last night and upgraded my phone. This one is my old one. Jayshawn can have it."

"Shut up," she said, her mouth dropping open in surprise, excited as if the phone was for her. "You did not. That's so nice of you."

My reasons for giving Jayshawn my old phone weren't entirely pure. I wanted to be able to call or text him regularly, and that wasn't possible when I had to wait until he was on Wi-Fi. I wanted him to have what other kids his age had—on top of the fact that I owed him 15 years of birthdays.

I pulled the cellphone out of the bag to show her I wasn't lying.

"Let me see," she said, reaching for the box the phone came in. "Girls, one of you go inside and grab Jayshawn. Oh, he's going to be so happy you got him a phone."

She'd asked one of her daughters to go get him, but they all ran back toward the front door, screaming Jayshawn's name and yelling for him to come outside.

"Your mother got you a phone!" I heard one of them shout.

It didn't take long for him to come out, with TJ at his side. Destiny handed him the phone, which he gladly took, and he walked around to my yellow Jeep and got in. He gave me a side hug as a thank-you for the gift.

"TJ wants to come too," he said. It was not a question. It was a statement—he was telling me. I looked at Destiny to see her response.

"You can go, Bugs," she said to TJ, who didn't need to be told twice.

"I just wanted to come out and meet you before he left with you, you know?" She chuckled and took another drag. "Make sure you're not some kind of crackhead or psycho."

Crackhead, I understood. But how would she know if I was a psycho?

"I get it," I said, trying to sound understanding. Jayshawn clearly meant a lot to her, and I wanted her to know that I recognized that. I was sure he wished she was his mother, but hopefully, after meeting me, that would change. Being jealous of her bond with Jayshawn was ridiculous, and I knew that. Still, my brain and heart weren't on the same page. The close bond they had was something I could have had with him. It was something I had with his half-brother, and I wanted it with him too.

***

When we arrived back at the house, Mendel was waiting at the door to greet us.

"Hey. I made you dinner," he said, stepping aside to let us in.

"Say less. I'm starving," I replied.

"Well, you're in for a treat—three courses tonight," he said with a grin.

I set the table and grabbed a bottle of wine from the counter before sitting down. Jayshawn and TJ joined us, looking curiously at the setup.

"Your mom tells me you play football," Mendel said, addressing Jayshawn, who was about to take a bite of brisket.

"Yeah, I did. But not anymore. I hurt my hip, and I need physical therapy."

So, on top of everything else, he's not getting proper medical care, I thought, biting back my frustration.

"You guys always have this large spread for dinner?" TJ asked.

"Well, not entirely. We have a big meal every Friday night. It's called Shabbat dinner. Mendel is Jewish, and I'm about to convert soon, actually."

"Oh, okay."

"Wait, so y'all don't celebrate Christmas?" Jayshawn asked, looking surprised.

"Nope. Hanukkah."

"Wow. Eight nights of gifts is pretty cool," he said with a small smile.

We finished dinner, which Jayshawn quickly devoured, while TJ nibbled at his food. Afterward, I turned on the TV in the living room, and the boys went to the spare bedroom to play video games.

The days continued to pass, with Jayshawn and TJ coming over regularly. Sometimes, they even stayed the night. His "mother" didn't seem to notice or care where he was. If she did ask, he would simply say he was at TJ's house, and that would be the end of it.

Even though we'd been seeing each other for weeks, I didn't want to cancel the first meeting Vivian had planned for me and Jayshawn at Christmas. Doing so might cause suspicion. She might wonder why Jayshawn or I had suddenly lost interest in meeting.

Here I was, getting dressed for Christmas at Vanity's, preparing to act like this was the first time I was meeting "Mo." I'd have to pretend we hadn't been spending time together for months—having dinners, spending weekends together, or even celebrating my birthday just three days ago at Topgolf with Charlie, TJ, and my friends Kaila and Shia.

Not only would I have to act surprised and emotional, as if seeing my son for the first time in 15 years, but I'd also have to play nice. Pretend Vivian was doing me a favor by arranging this meeting and allowing me to have a relationship with him.

I just hoped she didn't say anything implying that, because I didn't know if I'd be able to contain myself. If she did, I might end up letting the entire room know how her sister, her mother, and Vivian herself had taken advantage of a 15-year-old girl and never kept their word. The whole event could quickly become awkward and ugly.

I didn't like confrontation, though, so as long as Vivian acted cordial, I planned to do the same.

It was dark when we arrived, and based on the number of cars lining the street, we were the last to get there. Mendel and I got out of the car and walked up the pathway, where people I didn't recognize were mingling outside the doorway. Probably cousins I'd never met. I walked past them without saying a word.

The house was different from the one Vanity lived in when I was in her care, but it was cluttered all the same. African art adorned the walls, elephant figurines crowded end tables, and a large Christmas tree stood in the corner, almost behind the sofa Vanity was sitting on. With the house so cluttered and cramped, I was surprised she'd managed to find space for the tree at all.

Vanity's youngest daughter, Kianna, sat next to her with her two small children standing at her feet. Directly across from her sat her second-oldest daughter, Tashia, with her two children clinging to her. Vivian sat on the opposite sofa next to an older white man I didn't recognize. Sitting on the floor in front of an old TV was Jayshawn.

I walked past Vivian without acknowledging her and instead directed my attention to Vanity.

"Hello," I said. Vanity had her faults, but oddly, I didn't harbor the same hate for her as I did for Vivian. Pretending to make nice with Vivian wasn't going to happen. She was a shady liar. Then again, so was I now, having gone behind her back to build a relationship with Jayshawn.

"Hi, I'm Nicole's fiancé, Mendel," he said, introducing himself.

"Hi! Sit down, sit down," Vanity said, looking up smiling and waving her hand as if she were hosting some grand event.

I decided to sit on the floor next to Jayshawn. He had a few gifts in front of him, none of which looked thoughtful at all. Most were hygiene products. Hygiene products were not Christmas gifts; they were necessities.

I tried to make small talk with him, asking about the games he'd been playing and whether he'd received everything he wanted for Christmas. But I felt watched and didn't want to say too much. Showing up at all felt like a mistake. I felt out of place. Vanity carried on as if nothing was odd, as if we were all one big happy family.

"I need someone to peel the eggs for the deviled eggs," Vanity announced.

They hadn't eaten dinner yet. Typical. I shouldn't have been surprised. Vanity did everything on her own time.

"I'll do it," I blurted out, eager to escape the room.

I got up and headed to the kitchen. I hated to cook in a dirty kitchen, so the small, cramped, and cluttered space made me uncomfortable, but sitting on the floor, surrounded by people I didn't want to talk to, was worse. By the time I finished peeling the eggs, all the presents had been exchanged.

I handed Jayshawn the card Mendel and I had picked up on the way to Vanity's.

"There's a $50 gift card inside for you to get yourself something," I said in a low voice. "We're going to head out now," I announced to the room.

"I'll walk you out," Jayshawn said.

As we reached the door, I saw Vivian glance at us. I hoped she didn't suspect anything. I wasn't entirely sure I'd acted like someone meeting their son for the first time. I hadn't asked him any questions, hadn't acted surprised. Even if it had truly been our first meeting, I wouldn't have asked questions in front of an audience.

"Who was that older white man sitting next to Kianna?" I asked once we were out of earshot, whispering out of habit.

"Oh, that's her client Craig."

"So what, he lives with her?"

"Yeah, he's, like, special needs, and she takes care of him."

"Good grief," I muttered. So she'd switched from fostering children poorly to caring for disabled adults.

I had wondered if she had continued to foster youth after everything that went down with me getting pregnant and repeatedly ditching school and running away.

"Give your son a hug," Mendel said, holding out his phone to snap a picture of us.

"Make sure your flash is on. We don't glow in the dark like you," I joked.

"The flash is on," he said, snapping a few photos.

"Let me see, let me see," I said, reaching for the camera. "Jayshawn, you're not smiling in any of these."

"I don't really like to smile because of my gap."

"Jayshawn, you're a handsome kid—gap and all," I said as I got into the car. "I'll call you later."

Mic Check

"Hey," I greeted Jayshawn as he got into my Jeep. "Sorry you had to wait so long. There was traffic."

Nothing Vivian or Vanity had said to me had changed anything. I continued to pick up Jayshawn as often as he would let me, always behind her back. I knew sneaking around with a child might look wrong, but he was my son, and things were complicated.

"It's cool," he said.

"You hungry?" I asked.

"Yeah. My buddy wants to come too."

"Where do y'all want to eat?"

"There's a burger joint down the street near his house."

"Okay."

"You're gonna turn right after the light up ahead, then just go straight for a while. His house is gonna be on the left."

I made the turn. "So, you told him you were adopted, or what?"

"I pretty much told everybody. I was so shocked."

I sighed. "Dang. What did he say?"

"Well, he was shocked, like me."

I pulled onto his friend's block. The neighborhood was nice, with large homes, two-car garages, and well-kept lawns.

"Just stop here," Jayshawn told me when we were halfway down the block. "I'll walk the rest of the way. I'm not tryna have his mom tell my mom I'm meeting with you."

After it got out that I had met up with Jayshawn before Christmas—and that I was the one buying him teenage essentials—both Vivian and Vanity had confronted me over text. I didn't care to repeat that experience.

"No problem," I said, pulling over and parking carefully to avoid blocking anyone's driveway.

Jayshawn got out of the car and crossed the street. He wasn't in the house long before he came back out, followed by a thinner, shorter boy.

"Hey, I'm Johny," the kid said as he slid into the back seat with Jayshawn. "You're Jayshawn's real mom, huh?" He smirked like he knew we were sneaking around and was thrilled to be in on the secret.

"So, Jayshawn tells me you two play football together," I said, glancing at Johny in the rearview mirror.

"Yeah," Johny replied.

"So, other than football, what else do you boys like to do for fun?"

"Rap," Johny said.

"Oh, you guys rap?" I asked, thinking about how I used to write poetry in my group homes. I decided not to mention my failed attempt at singing—hearing my voice on playback had made me scratch that as a career idea.

"Yeah. I recorded sometimes with my godbrother Darius, but I ain't never been to an actual studio or nothing," Jayshawn said.

"Have you been to a studio?" I asked Johny.

"Nah. I wish," he replied.

The McDonald's was one of the larger ones, with a playground and plenty of seating, including booths and tables. While we stood in line to order, the boys noticed a group of classmates sitting at a booth in the back.

"Yo, Jamal!" Johny yelled.

"Oh shit. Sup, y'all?" Jamal replied.

I ordered food for myself, Jayshawn, and Johny. The boys joined their friends to wait for their orders while I sat at a nearby table, devouring my fries three at a time. After about an hour, they were ready to leave.

Before heading out, their friends stopped by my table to introduce themselves and say goodbye. I smiled, nodding as they left.

I stopped the car a few houses down from where Johny lived, not too worried about being seen since it was already dark outside.

"You know, I remember James was always rapping," I told Jayshawn. "Him and this guy named Point."

"Yeah, that's my daddy's cousin," Jayshawn replied.

"I've never been to a studio either. It'd be cool to see what it looks like, you know."

"Shit, say less," Jayshawn said.

I grabbed my phone and searched for recording studios nearby. The first few places were fully booked and offered appointments for another day. Impatient to do something exciting, I expanded my search to our current location instead of just Phoenix.

Saltmine Studio popped up first on the list. It was 12 minutes away and had a 4.7-star rating. I called the number and followed the prompts.

"Saltmine Studios, this is Don," a man answered.

"Hi, Don. I was hoping to get into the studio today if you have slots available."

"Do you have a room in mind?" he asked.

"No, this would be our first time," I replied.

"Okay. Let me check and see what's available," he said, humming as he searched. "We have one room open at 7 p.m. It's $120 an hour with a two-hour minimum."

"We'll take the 7 p.m. time slot."

"Okay. I just need a card to hold your spot."

I grabbed my purse, pulled out my card, and read off the number. Once the call ended, I put the address into my GPS and started driving.

"So, where does your mother think you are?" I asked Jayshawn, knowing we wouldn't leave the studio until around 9 p.m.

"She didn't really ask where I was at. I guess she just assumed I was with TJ or Johny if I wasn't at my aunt's house."

"Aww."

The street where the studio was located didn't look like much, and I wouldn't have guessed there was a studio there. Jayshawn and I walked down the street, looking for signage, but instead, we saw a tall iron gate with a buzzer on a half wall beside it. A camera pointed down at us, with another facing the sidewalk.

I pressed the buzzer. A voice came over the speaker. "Can I help you?"

"We have a 7 p.m. session," I said. The gate started sliding open before I could finish, and Jayshawn and I walked in.

The place was massive, like a private compound in the middle of the city. Three buildings sat on the property, with the largest in the center. The two smaller buildings looked like cabins. A sports car was parked near one of the smaller buildings, which had a water fountain in front. Near the other was an outdoor fireplace, where a few people sat smoking. Closer to the main building, some guys played ping pong under heat lamps. Off to the right were steps leading to a sitting area with vending machines against the wall.

"Wow," I said to Jayshawn. "I would've never expected all this."

"Right? I wanna know whose car that is," Jayshawn said.

The door to the main building opened just before I could touch it.

"Nice to see you found the place. I'm Don," said an older man with short grayish-white hair.

"Thanks."

"This place is crazy," Jayshawn added.

"Follow me, and I'll show you around," Don said.

Don led us through the main building, starting with a wall showcasing photos of famous artists who'd recorded at the studio. I stared in disbelief as I recognized some of the faces.

"I can't believe artists come all the way to Mesa to record," I said.

"Well, this is one of the only luxury recording studios in the Valley," Don explained, clearly proud of the facility.

"I thought famous and wealthy people preferred Scottsdale," I joked.

Don chuckled. "We have something Scottsdale doesn't—world-class sound and privacy. That's why they come here."

He continued the tour, pointing out a spacious kitchen, a lounge area with a massive couch and TV, and a few smaller rooms that served as rehearsal spaces.

Eventually, he brought us to the studio we'd be using. The room was dimly lit, with a plush sofa along the back wall. In front of it was the engineer's setup—an elaborate desk with a computer, keyboard, and a dizzying array of buttons and knobs. Massive speakers hung from the walls, and the entire room felt like it was designed to absorb sound.

"This is where the magic happens," Don said, gesturing to the equipment. Then he opened a door I hadn't noticed before. "And this," he added, "is the recording booth."

The booth was small but well-lit, with a microphone suspended in the center. Thick, soundproof walls surrounded it, and I could tell just by looking at it that it was designed to block out every noise imaginable.

"It's completely soundproof in there," Don explained to Jayshawn. "You won't hear anything except what's coming through the headphones. But we'll be able to hear you loud and clear from this side."

"Cool," Jayshawn said, stepping closer to get a better look.

At that moment, the engineer walked in—a man in his 30s with long dreadlocks and a friendly smile.

"Hey, I'm Kyle," he said, shaking our hands. "You must be Jayshawn."

"Yeah," Jayshawn said, his excitement starting to show.

Kyle sat down at the computer and pulled up a blank recording session. "Do you already have a beat, or do you want to pick one out here?" he asked.

"Yeah, I got one," Jayshawn said, scrolling through his phone. He quickly emailed it to Kyle, who downloaded it and began setting everything up.

"Okay," Kyle said after a few minutes. "Go ahead and step into the booth, and we'll get started."

Jayshawn glanced at me, his nerves showing for just a second, before stepping into the booth. I couldn't help but smile. This moment felt surreal, like something out of a TV show.

Inside the booth, Jayshawn adjusted the headphones and looked back through the glass at Kyle, who gave him a thumbs-up.

"Say something into the mic so I can check the levels," Kyle said.

"Yo, yo, mic check," Jayshawn said, his voice coming through the speakers in the control room. It was crisp and clear, and I could tell he was already feeling more confident.

Kyle made a few adjustments, then played the beat Jayshawn had selected. It filled the room, deep and rhythmic, and Jayshawn began nodding his head to the music.

"All right, we're ready when you are," Kyle said.

Jayshawn took a deep breath, closed his eyes for a moment, and then began to rap. His voice was steady and deliberate, flowing effortlessly over the beat. I was impressed—not just by his skill but by the confidence he exuded.

I grabbed my phone and started snapping pictures, then switched to recording a video. I wanted him to remember this moment forever, his first time in a real studio.

After a couple of takes, Kyle played back the recording, and Jayshawn leaned out of the booth to listen. He nodded approvingly as he heard his voice, clear and polished, over the track.

"This is dope," he said, grinning.

"You've got talent, man," Kyle replied. "Keep working on your craft, and you could go far."

Jayshawn stepped out of the booth, and I could see the pride on his face. I knew I couldn't rewind time or make up for the years we'd missed, but moments like this—creating new memories together—felt like a step in the right direction.

"Thank you for doing this," Jayshawn said as we walked back to the car.

Family Moment

One of Mendel's clients—a football player he'd recently helped get into a house—had given him free tickets to a game. It had been a great time, except for the fact that I wore a jean jacket instead of an actual coat. Sitting in the outdoor winter air, I was freezing. By the time the game was over, my chest was tight, and I desperately needed my inhaler.

My asthma put a dent in my plan to party it up in Old Town with Kaila, Shia, and maybe Mendel. He liked to work major holidays since people drinking often meant they became forgetful and needed locksmiths. Instead, I drove to Kaila's house, puffed my inhaler a few more times, and fell asleep on her couch. She still went out, though, and Mendel picked me up in the early hours of the morning. I crawled into bed and went right back to sleep. That was my New Year's Eve.

I reached for my phone on the nightstand and saw that it was already 11 a.m. I'd slept the morning away. Checking my emails, I saw that the listing agent still hadn't gotten back to me about the purchase offer I'd submitted for my client. After deleting some junk emails, I tapped the green chat bubble on my phone, which let me know I had ten unread messages. It was New Year's Day, so I figured most of them were "Happy New Year" messages.

Among the well-wishes, I noticed messages from both Vanity and Vivian. I decided to open Vanity's first.

Vanity: Well…Nicole, he's 15 and all excited about his interactions with you, but next time, you need to tell him you'll talk to Vivian and see if she says it's okay! He could have gotten a phone for Christmas or earned it for good grades at the end of the semester! We all need to discuss these things because he doesn't need to keep asking for things when he's just meeting you! He's a kid, but still, there's a proper way to do things. We all need to communicate and work together!

Welp, I thought. I guess they figured out it was me who bought him the PlayStation and gave him a cellphone.

Fuck. This kid could not keep a damn secret to save his life.

I reread Vanity's message, shaking my head. Next time, I need to tell him to talk to Vivian? Sure, in what fucking world? I muttered to myself, rolling my eyes. I didn't bother responding. If Vanity or Vivian had any plans to get Jayshawn a phone, they would have done so already. And the fact that Vanity thought this was somehow a "we" situation that involved her was classic Vanity.

I clicked out of her message and opened Vivian's.

Vivian: Nicole, I did want to talk to you and tell you that it's disrespectful to do things behind my back, like meeting up with my son without my knowledge. You doing that undermines my authority. From here on out, if you're going to give him money or want to spend time with him, I need to know about it ahead of time. This is new territory for all of us, and the situation is a little awkward. It can also be confusing, especially for a kid or teenager. So please let me know when you want to do something, and we can make it happen TOGETHER, or I can give permission for it to be okay. Nothing should be going on without my consent. That's just respect—woman to woman, mother to mother. I hope you can understand where I'm coming from. It's all LOVE.

Now she talks about togetherness. Now there's a "we," and she suddenly knew how to communicate.

I reread the message a couple of times, trying to think of a response.

Jayshawn was a minor, and the courts had placed him under her care. If this were any other child or any other situation, I would have been in the wrong. I would have apologized for going behind her back. But Jayshawn was my child, and this wasn't any other circumstance.

I birthed him.

And what the hell did she mean by "mother to mother"? Did she seriously think that phrase would make us bond or come to some mutual understanding? Because that was never going to happen. In my mind, she might as well have been a kidnapper.

There was no equal ground.

No shared motherhood.

No understanding between us.

There was no "mother to mother" fifteen years ago when she ghosted me. There was no respect for me as a mother when she moved and cut me off from my son.

I clicked out of her message without responding. Now that Jayshawn had a phone, I didn't need her permission to speak to him. I had no respect for Vivian or Vanity, and I would never ask her permission to spend time with my son.

She clearly wasn't that hands-on anyway. She didn't even know where Jayshawn was right now—in my spare bedroom with his best friend, TJ, and his stepbrother, Charlie. All three boys were packed and ready for our family skiing trip to Mount Lemmon in Tucson.

Charlie had arrived the day after Christmas since me and Mendel didn't celebrate and didn't want Charlie to have to be deprived of the event.

The boys were a bit squished in the back of my yellow Jeep, but it was fine. They were tired anyway, probably because they'd stayed up playing games all night. Charlie, sitting on the end, had his head on Jayshawn's shoulder. Jayshawn was slumped over on TJ, and TJ had his head against the window. All three were sound asleep. I couldn't pass up the chance to snap a couple of pictures. Having both my sons together and on a road trip made me unbelievably happy.

Jayshawn and TJ coming along on the trip had been a last-minute decision, but luckily, our hotel room had two queen beds and a sofa bed.

The next morning, after a quick hotel breakfast, we drove up the steep, winding mountain. The altitude was so high that both Jayshawn and I, who had asthma, felt like we were losing oxygen.

We rented skis and boots and watched a training video. Afterward, we took an hour-long class with a ski instructor, which had us all feeling confident enough to tackle the slopes. That confidence quickly evaporated when all of us fell almost immediately after getting off the ski lift.

Falling on the practice run had been easy to recover from, but falling on the actual slope? That was a different story. Getting up with skis on was nearly impossible. By the time I made it down, I was done. I had no desire to keep falling. The dense, icy snow hurt every time I hit the ground, and I didn't make a habit of continuing activities that hurt.

I also had a strong aversion to falling for real and breaking my damn collarbone.

The others didn't mind falling. Jayshawn, TJ, Charlie, and Mendel kept skiing. They were better than me and seemed to enjoy it. I stood on the wooden deck of the lodge, snapping as many photos of them in action as I could as they went up and down the slopes.

On the way back down the mountain, we stopped at a restaurant for dinner, then lingered a bit to go sledding and visit a gift shop. Finally, we made our way back to the hotel.

The next morning, after breakfast, we made the two-hour trip back to Phoenix. TJ and Jayshawn were dropped off at Destiny's house, and Charlie went to Kaila's to play games with her kids.

Blindsided

Mendel's busy night had finally slowed down, and we were heading home from a long day of opening car doors, house and apartment doors, and making car keys. It was funny because when I first met Mendel and he told me he was a locksmith, the first thing I thought was: how busy could a locksmith actually be? Like, how often did people actually lock themselves out or lose a key? Well, apparently, the answer was often.

The music playing through the car speaker was interrupted briefly by the ding of my phone. I grabbed it, saw my son Jayshawn texting me, and smiled.

Me: hey Jayshawn, you make it back home yet?

Jayshawn: hun?

Me: ???

Jayshawn: Whats your address?

"Jayshawn is texting me asking me for my address," I said to Mendel, whose attention was on the road. "Weird, right?"

"I don't know. Just because someone knows where you live doesn't mean they have your actual address," he said, still looking ahead.

"Yeah, but I gave him my address literally the first day he messaged me on social media," I said, not convinced. "Maybe it's not Jayshawn."

Me: Why do you need my address?

Jayshawn: I am filling out a job application.

Me: What job are you applying to?

Jayshawn: A few different fast food places near me.

"Maybe it is really Jayshawn. He said it's for a job application," I told Mendel.

"Nice, tell him he can use me as a reference."

When we made it back to the house, I heated up some leftovers for me and Mendel and opened a bottle of wine while he showered. When it came to selecting a movie to watch, I was pretty indecisive, but I managed to settle on a title just as Mendel entered the living room.

After placing a portion of leftover Chinese on each of our plates, he poured two glasses of wine, and we started the movie.

Knock.

Knock.

Knock.

I jumped up from where I'd been snuggled into Mendel, startled by the banging at our front door.

"Are you expecting company?"

The knocking continued in a flurry of explosions.

"No," he said, getting up from the sofa to answer the front door before it was completely knocked down by the person on the other side.

Slightly terrified, I stayed on the sofa, waiting for Mendel to reveal who was doing the angry banging.

The door was barely ajar when I heard yelling. I could tell it was a female voice, but I couldn't make out what she was saying.

My husband silently stood in the doorway as the woman continued to scream and shout.

Now curious, I got up from the sofa and approached the door.

It was an angry Vivian—and a shy Jayshawn cowering behind her.

"You sneaky snake bitch, you've been going behind my back!" her voice boomed, letting her rage for me rise. She took a step forward, her entire frame now in the doorway, forcing me and Mendel to step back.

I took several steps back until I was standing less in the living room and more in the kitchen. Vivian was huge and looked like she was itching for a fight I had no intention of giving her. She was an angry beast of a woman, and I knew one hit from her would have me laid out flat.

No thanks.

"Buying him a phone is one thing, but taking him out of town without my permission is just some slimy ass shit."

I couldn't believe she had the nerve to call me slimy after everything she had done.

Yeah, okay. I was the slimy one.

Vivian was still screaming and carrying on when Jayshawn slipped past her and entered the living room, plopping himself on the sofa.

Mendel then shut the door, and I raced to the living room window to see what she might do next—but she was already heading to her car. I watched out the window as she backed out of the driveway.

Why was she leaving?

She had to know Jayshawn was in the house and not in her car.

She had just been screaming her lungs out that I was a snake—and she drove off without Jayshawn.

"Wait, what did she say?" I asked Mendel. He was just as confused as I was. "Well, where did she go?"

Mendel stood at the kitchen counter in silence, just as baffled by the events that had just taken place.

"What the hell! Is she coming back?"

Jayshawn shook his head. "I don't think so," he said.

He looked sad, sitting slumped on the end piece of my sofa. Vivian wasn't his real mother, and he knew that now—but even still, rejection hurt. From my experience, it was almost worse being rejected by someone you were willing to essentially settle for. Like when a 10 decided to date a 4, and then the 4 had the audacity to end things like you weren't the catch.

Even though he knew she had lied about being his birth mother—to the point of making up an entire birth story, which was definitely certifiable in my opinion—he continued to speak with her and return home.

I had gone through something similar when my sister and I were dropped off unsuspectingly at the Department of Child Safety by our very much abusive adoptive parents. We should have been relieved and happy to be out of the care of people who physically and mentally mistreated us, but instead, we felt rejected, confused, sad, and alone.

Rather than act happy to finally have him in my home, I felt empathetic toward his feelings of probable shock and confusion.

"What just happened?" I asked. Everything had been going fine for months, so how we ended up in this moment was baffling to me too.

"My mom," Jayshawn started to say, and I cringed, "she just came up to me and asked for my phone."

"You didn't have a password on it?"

"I did. She asked me to give it to her, and I couldn't say no. She went through all the messages in my phone and was so pissed. I don't think I've ever seen her this angry. Then she started texting you as if she was me."

I fucking knew something was off about that goddamn text message. I should've trusted my intuition and ignored it.

"Mendel, I told you him asking for my address after being in our home a thousand times was odd, didn't I? Now look." I turned to Mendel, who was still standing in the kitchen while Jayshawn and I sat on the sofa. I think the entire thing had him overwhelmed.

That fucking bitch managed to play me again. I felt embarrassed that I was really sitting there texting her about a nonexistent job and Mendel being a reference. Ugh. I could not stand her.

"She read all the messages and knows I've been sneaking over to your house. She found out we went skiing."

"So in her rage, she decided to show up to my doorstep and then let you stay?" I asked, confused as to why she went through the trouble of screaming if she was just going to walk away without an actual fight. "This is wild. So does this mean she's handing you over to me? Where are your clothes?"

"Should we call her?" Mendel asked, earning a stare from both me and Jayshawn.

"No."

"Well, what are we supposed to do? She just showed up on a school night and left him here."

"Do you even have school tomorrow?" I asked Jayshawn. I didn't keep up with the holidays too much—maybe he was off school.

"Yeah," he answered.

"So we'll have to get you something to wear on the way to school," I said, looking over at Jayshawn. He was sitting slumped on the sofa and looked a little down. I wondered what she must've said to him on the car ride over to have him in such a slump.

Vivian wasn't his real mother anyway, and as far as I could tell, hadn't actually treated him well, so why he was sitting on the sofa looking like a wounded animal escaped me. Sure, he snuck behind her back, but I was his mother. She was just the woman who managed to legally kidnap him from me. He shouldn't be sad at her reaction to him wanting to meet me—he should've been angry that he had never met me and felt the need to sneak and do it in the first place.

"Do you want to live with me?" I asked Jayshawn.

"Yeah."

"Okay, well, it's late, I'm tired, and you have school in the morning," I said, standing. "What time is school so I can set an alarm?"

"7:15 a.m."

"Oh yeah, goodnight then." I hadn't woken up that early since being a ward of the state.

Confrontation

I pulled up to the main entrance of Jayshawn's school in Mesa. This marked the second time I had driven him to or picked him up from school since Vivian had dropped him off unannounced on Friday night. It was Monday now, and still, no word from her.

I spotted Jayshawn walking toward the car, but he wasn't alone. A petite girl with long black hair was walking beside him.

"Can you give my girlfriend a ride?" Jayshawn asked as they approached.

She looked at me sweetly, but Jayshawn already knew I'd say yes—I hadn't said no to him since we met.

"Yeah, hop in," I said, pressing the unlock button more times than necessary.

Jayshawn and his girlfriend slid into the backseat together. I waited until everyone was settled before pulling out of the school complex.

"Can I see your phone?" Jayshawn asked.

"Sure," I said. I knew he didn't have a phone anymore since Vivian had taken it a few nights ago and still hadn't returned it.

"I need your address to drop you off, hun," I said to the girl, glancing at her in the rearview mirror.

"It's the Evergreen Apartments," she said. "Just turn right up here."

"Okay." I turned, then glanced in the rearview mirror again and saw Jayshawn still on my phone.

"Who are you texting anyway?" I asked, wanting my phone back. I preferred seeing and hearing the GPS on the car monitor and wanted to link my phone to it.

"My mom—" Jayshawn started, then corrected himself, "I mean, Vivian. I'm asking about getting my things."

"Let me see. What is she saying?" I asked, reaching for the phone.

He hesitated but handed it over.

"I was just asking her about getting my things and moving to Phoenix," he sputtered out.

I looked at the screen and felt my stomach sink.

Me: I want to enroll him in school. In Phoenix. Do you think I can do that, or do I need to go to court and get guardianship?

"Jayshawn!" I exclaimed in horror. "Why would you say that? And as me? She thinks I'm saying this! You shouldn't have used my phone this way." My voice rose, frustration spilling out. I would have never threatened her with guardianship like that. I kept scrolling to see Vivian's response.

Vivian: He is already enrolled in school. Yeah, go and get guardianship.

Me: Why are you mad about him just getting to know me? It wasn't anything serious.

Vivian: That's what you fucking fail to realize. It's not about YOU. But because you're a sneaky, lying-ass bitch, you're trying to make it that way. BUT honey, do what you want—you've been doing it since you met. I was the fool for thinking we were better than that!!!

I kept reading, my anger rising with every word.

Me: All I can say is thank you.

Vivian: The least you can do is encourage him to do the right thing and go to school. If you can handle that, maybe he can change later. But for now, take him or give him bus money so he can finish his education and NOT end up in juvie or a dumbass group home BECAUSE OF YOU. And yes, you're WELCOME.

My vision blurred with rage.

A liar? Juvie? Group home? Education? Who did she think she was? I hadn't finished high school, but I earned my GED and went on to get my master's degree. And now she wanted to insinuate I was incapable of encouraging my own son?

Vivian: And for the record I never did or said anything bad about you to try and make everything as easy as possible for him as always but you wanted to do the wrong thing over and over again because of who you are so do what you have to do I know God will take care of him regardless.

I pressed the small mic icon on my phone activating voice-to-text because I couldn't stop driving, but I had far too much to say to type it all out.

Me: I gave Jayshawn my phone to take to school, so you were speaking with him. I'll need the phone I got him back though. Thanks. And after reading these messages, I realize you've lost your mind. I know you aren't trying to call me bad because I was in a group home—NO FAULT OF MY OWN—but because your neglectful mother fucking mother was too busy laid up with several men to realize what was happening under her own roof. And you date criminals and felons. Jayshawn tells me your boyfriend now is doing time in Tucson. While you're putting money on his books, Jayshawn is out here stealing from corner stores. You and your entire family are LOW-LIFE THUGS.

She hadn't responded yet, but I couldn't stop now. I was on a roll. She thought she had been playing nice. My fingers trembled, and my mouth ran dry. I had held back for so long, trying not to seem bitter, trying not to rock the boat. Well, not anymore. She needed to know how much I hated her.

Me: "What happened to your motherfucking marriage, bitch, huh? Oh, and I heard you were mistreating Jayshawn. And let's address the lying, sneaky part—I didn't need YOUR permission to see the son I BIRTHED. Don't forget to tell me where I could pick up my phone, because I WAS going to do that."

Vivian: "Little girl. MY SON ain't never been mistreated, so you could say whatever the fuck you wanted. You didn't know me or him."

Me: "He told me you hit him. Kicked him out in the cold with no shoes. Should I go on?"

Vivian: "You're a liar, so who gave a fuck what you thought or what anybody ever told you. YOU AIN'T SHIT, BITCH. FUCK YOU."

Me: "Except YOU were the liar. Failing to tell him he was adopted? Pretending you were his biological mother and that your ass was really in the hospital? You were a pathetic-ass bitch."

Vivian: "lol"

Me: "Yeah, it's real funny."

Vivian: "Amen to that."

I slammed the phone face-down in my lap, finally focusing on the road again.

"Fuck her," I muttered. "You want to live with me and switch schools? You want to get your things from YOUR house? Fine. Okay. You didn't need her permission. It was done. We'd get your things. What's your address?"

Reclaiming My Son

I pulled my yellow Jeep into the five-unit complex Jayshawn shared with Vivian and got out. Jayshawn walked around the back of his unit, checking if his bedroom window was unlocked, but the entire apartment was locked up tight.

Luckily, with Mendel owning a locksmith company, this was no problem for me. I called him to ask if he had a locksmith in the Mesa area who could meet me at Jayshawn's apartment.

Turned out, an independent contractor named Daniel was in the area and could be there in 15 minutes.

When Daniel arrived, it took him less than a minute to unlock the door. Before I knew it, I was stepping into Jayshawn's apartment, his girlfriend trailing behind me.

The apartment was small but nicely decorated and spotless. Pictures of abstract artwork, rather than personal photos, hung on the walls. A small black loveseat sat against the back wall under blackout shades, with a fluffy rug beneath a glass coffee table. A TV rested on a sleek stand against the opposite wall. The kitchen, with its open layout, was to the left of the living room. There wasn't a single dish in the sink or on the countertops. The entire space was so pristine, it felt staged—like a model home, not a place where people actually lived.

I followed Jayshawn down the narrow hallway, glancing into the hall bathroom as we passed. Like the rest of the apartment, it was immaculate. The toilet seat was down, with a fuzzy cover that matched the bathmats and hand towels.

I had to give it to her—Vivian had taste. She'd managed to make a rundown apartment in Mesa look charming and immaculate on the inside. If I didn't despise the woman, I'd have asked her how she managed to decorate and keep such a prestige home.

The next room we came to, though, was Jayshawn's.

His room was the stark opposite of the rest of the apartment. It was barren. No dresser. No wall art. No posters. No clothes tossed around like you'd expect in a teenager's room. The only piece of furniture was a full-size bed propped up on cinder blocks.

Literally cinder blocks.

Not even a bed frame.

His closet held only his backpack, a few beat-up sneakers, and maybe 10 to 15 articles of clothing, most of which looked like they were bought at a swap meet.

This was absolute bullshit.

Did she ever even love him? His living space resembled a juvenile detention center. This was not the room of a loved teenager.

"Clear out the closet," I told Jayshawn, my voice tight with barely restrained anger. "Don't leave anything fucking behind in this place."

"I don't want everything," he said hesitantly. "A lot of the clothes I don't even wear."

"Doesn't matter," I snapped.

I started pulling clothes off hangers, grabbing as much as I could carry, and throwing it all into the trunk of my Jeep. Jayshawn stared at me, stunned and frozen in place.

"I want her to know you left," I explained as I passed him in the hallway on another trip to his room. "I want her to see that you took all your shit and you're not coming back."

This woman and her family had caused me nothing but pain. It was time for her to feel a little of that. The son she stole and raised as her own—and possibly loved in her own twisted way—was rejecting her completely.

All her lies, built over 15 years, had finally unraveled. She was being exposed for the crazy woman she'd always been. Lifetime movie special crazy.

I wanted this win.

My son, who lived with her his entire life, met me and immediately said yes to moving in with me—a stranger he'd known for barely six months.

It showed just how "loved" he must have actually felt in her cookie-cutter home.

Five trips later, I'd cleared out everything but the bed from Jayshawn's room. I did a final once-over to make sure I hadn't missed anything and headed toward the front door.

"Wait," Jayshawn said suddenly.

"What?" I stopped walking and turned to face him.

"I want to show you the adoption paperwork I found." He walked into Vivian's room, and I followed.

Her bedroom was as neat and decorated as the rest of the house. The bed looked similar in size to Jayshawn's, except it was in a sleek white bed frame. A large dresser with a vanity mirror sat against the wall, lined with pictures of friends or family members. Jayshawn appeared in only one of them—he looked about six years old in the photo.

Had she not taken a single picture of him worth printing and framing since then?

The urge to tear her room apart and destroy its tidy perfection overwhelmed me. But I held back, watching as Jayshawn pulled a large box from the top of her closet and placed it on the bed.

He opened it carefully and pulled out a manila envelope stamped "CONFIDENTIAL" in bright red letter's.

Well, if that didn't scream "open me" to anyone snooping, I didn't know what did.

If she had never planned on telling Jayshawn he was adopted, why keep this paperwork? Without it, he would have had no way of knowing he wasn't her biological child—outside of a DNA test or me tracking him down when he turned 18.

The thought formed a pit in my stomach. I took a few deep breaths to steady myself.

"I think it's funny she'd keep something this big—this life-changing—in her closet," I said to Jayshawn, anger seeping into my voice. She had literally made up a whole birthing story, which for the life of me I could not get over. Who in their right mind did that? She needed help.

The urge to trash her room resurfaced, but I pushed it down. Clearing out Jayshawn's room would have to be enough of a statement.

On our way out, I twisted the front door handle lock from the inside, leaving the apartment just as pristine as we had found it.

We got back into my Jeep, and I drove Jayshawn's girlfriend home. He got out with her.

"I'm going to hang out here for a while," he said.

"Okay," I replied. "I'm not driving back out here tonight, so make sure you have everything you need."

He nodded, and I watched as they walked toward her building. Then I pulled away, my Jeep loaded with his belongings, and headed back home.

By the time I pulled into my driveway, the adrenaline from earlier had finally started to wear off, leaving me exhausted. I sat in the Jeep for a moment, staring at the pile of Jayshawn's things in the back. The events of the day replayed in my mind—Vivian's lies, Jayshawn's barren room, and the box of adoption papers stamped "CONFIDENTIAL."

It was too much. I took a deep breath, stepped out of the Jeep, and headed inside. Mendel was on the couch, still in his work clothes, scrolling through his phone.

"How'd it go?" he asked, looking up.

"Exhausting," I said, kicking off my shoes. "But I got everything of his out of her apartment. And I mean everything." I flopped down beside him, sighing heavily. "You should've seen his room, Mendel. No dresser, no posters—just a bed on cinder blocks."

Mendel raised an eyebrow. "Seriously?"

"Yeah," I said, shaking my head. "The rest of the apartment was immaculate, like a catalog, but his room? It was like a jail cell."

Mendel's jaw tightened. "That's messed up."

"It really is." I paused, staring at the ceiling. "You know, she had photos everywhere. Not one of Jayshawn except one of him as a little kid. It's like he was just… an afterthought in his own house."

Mendel didn't respond, but his silence said everything.

"I asked him if he wanted to live with me," I continued, sitting up. "And he said yes."

"Of course he did. You're his mom."

I smiled faintly. "Yeah, well, now we just have to figure out what comes next. When she comes home, she'll hopefully see all his stuff gone. I'm sure she's going to blow up my phone."

Mendel shrugged. "Let her."

***

I put Jayshawn's belongings in the spare bedroom, making a couple of trips back and forth to my trunk. As I finished unloading, my phone dinged in my pocket, letting me know it was at 10% battery. I placed it on the charger that was always plugged in at the edge of the kitchen counter near the sink and walked away. Opening the fridge, I scanned my dinner options and decided on a pasta and chicken dish.

Buzz. Buzz.

My phone vibrated on the counter. I had a text message from a Tucson area code. Opening the message, I read:

Vivian: Ooooh, y'all committing robbery NOW. I know y'all broke into my house while I was at work. My neighbors told me they saw a Mexican girl, a Black girl, and a Black guy entering my home and carrying things out. And I'm so fuckin' happy—I just gave the police all your info, and I will be pressing charges on both of y'all. Yep. Robbery is a felony.

Shit. Shit. Shit.

Maybe I had gone too far. I expected an argument, not the police.

Damn it.

I had wanted her to know we were there and to feel a sense of loss—hence why I had Jayshawn empty his entire room. This way, she wouldn't be able to question whether he was coming back or if things were actually missing.

But I didn't want to end up in jail.

I had really poked the bear this time.

I suppressed my rising fear. Maybe she was just angry and bluffing.

Me: You can't break into your own home. I picked Jayshawn up from school, and he asked if I could take him to HIS house to pick up his clothing.

I stared at my phone, waiting to see how she'd respond. Nothing came. I placed it back on the counter and plugged it in.

Buzz. Buzz.

Of course, just as I walked away, my phone rang. It was an unknown number. I hesitated. One ring. Two rings. Three.

The caller was lucky—I hated missed calls.

"Hello?"

"Hi, I'm Officer Gabriel Rodriguez with the Phoenix Police Department. Is this Nicole Hayes?"

"Yesssssss?" I drew out the word, feeling my stomach tighten.

You've got to be kidding me. Since when did the police work this fast? Vivian had texted me not 15 minutes ago, and now a detective was calling?

"She's filed a runaway report with the Mesa Police Department, naming Jayshawn Alexander as a missing person."

"What?!" I almost yelled. "He's not missing! She drove him to my house last Thursday."

The detective was silent, probably shocked by the blatant lie in the report. I pressed on. "She knows exactly where he is."

"Well," the officer replied sternly, "she's asked him to come home. Until he does, he will have to remain a missing person."

"She took his only form of communication," I retorted. "How is he supposed to contact her?"

"If Jayshawn is with you," he said, his tone firmer now, "or if you know where he is, I suggest you tell us to avoid being charged with harboring a runaway."

At that very moment, Jayshawn wasn't with me. He had arrived, but Destiny had picked him up less than 20 minutes earlier. Sometimes, Jayshawn enjoyed the quiet of my home, but other times, he missed the chaos of Destiny's house—after all, he had grown up with her nine kids since he was ten years old.

"Well, he isn't with me right now," I said matter-of-factly, keeping my voice steady despite the rising tension. "He's at a friend's house."

"What's the friend's name?"

"I don't know," I lied. I wasn't going to make this easy for him. "I'm sure Vivian can provide a list of all his friends," I snapped, then hung up before he could reply.

The stress of the call had me pacing my kitchen like I'd just downed an entire energy drink. Vivian was a skilled liar—I had to give her that. She had always managed to outsmart me, deceiving everyone around her with her manipulative ways.

Enough was enough.

Guardianship Wars

The phone connected after just one ring.

"Thank you for calling the Arizona Department of Child Safety. If you are calling regarding suspected abuse, neglect, exploitation, or abandonment of a child, please press 1."

I pressed one on my keypad.

"Please be advised a person who makes a false report is guilty of a class one misdemeanor," the audio recording stated.

I wasn't in the least bit worried about this because, unlike Vivian, I didn't just create entire stories out of thin air. If anything, I wished the police department had a recording like this that callers had to listen to before making a report—and that they actually enforced the rule by arresting liars like Vivian.

Five minutes elapsed before I heard a female voice greet me with a hello and ask the nature of my call. I tried my best to explain the situation.

"It's kind of a long story," I warned her before I began telling her the details.

"Jayshawn is my biological son who was adopted but had recently reached out to me to get to know me and forge a relationship. His adoptive mother, after learning about our meeting up and spending time together, dropped him off at my doorstep—angry—with no explanation. I went ahead and took him to school the next day and learned that he used my cell phone to tell her he no longer wanted to live with her and would not be returning. He had also mentioned as much to me the night he was dropped off. So I took him to get his belongings from his and her home and brought them to my house. Later in the evening, I learned she had reported him as a runaway to the police despite the fact that she had dropped him off at my house six days ago."

I paused to catch my breath, having rushed through the history as quickly as I could, knowing it was a lot of information.

"Anyway," I continued, "even prior to this event, I learned from my son that she often didn't leave food in the fridge and that he steals food from corner stores or waits to eat at a friend's. When I saw his room, it was pretty much bare, and most of his clothing is stolen."

The woman was silent during my entire explanation and finally spoke once I finished.

"I think, given the circumstances and the complicated relationship, we should set up a meeting with both you and Jayshawn, and his school counselor."

This was not what I wanted to hear.

Seriously. A meeting?

This woman dropped my son off at my doorstep in a rage—with no clothing and no real explanation as to why.

I wanted him removed from her care and placed in mine. If anything, that's what Child Protective Services was known for: removing children from their homes. But when I called them now, it was let's have a mediation and work things out.

I thought more about the idea of a mediation with Vivian. I didn't think it was the best idea. Vivian didn't want to sit down and have a discussion with me. She hated me. Besides, I wanted Child Protective Services to remove him from her care altogether and place him with me, so a mediation felt pointless. Really. When the hell did they stop taking children anyway? The day I needed them to. Now they wanted to sit down and have a meeting and work out a family plan.

I gave the woman on the line Vivian's number and the name of the school Jayshawn attended in Mesa so she could set up the meeting for the following day.

It was late in the afternoon when I heard from the Child Protective office again. They had assigned a caseworker to his case, and that was who would be showing up to the school tomorrow after his classes ended.

***

Westwood High School was fairly large, so I was shocked when I entered the counselor's office and saw how small it was. It felt like I had stepped into a closet rather than an office space. The room was rectangular in shape, and there was a desk pushed against a wall in the back, file cabinets lined the right side of the wall, and on the opposite side were a pair of chairs. I sat down in one while Jayshawn remained standing, leaning against the wall near the door.

His body language made me think the idea of having to have a conversation with his mother and me made him nervous. I was a bit nervous too, considering our last encounter had been her screaming at me in the doorway of my home.

Vivian was late, and when the counselor dialed her number, the phone rang and rang before finally going to voicemail.

My dilemma of him not wanting to go back home, but also being a runaway—coupled with harboring a runaway being a crime—still remained. That, and the fact that I didn't want to say hey dude, I'm sorry—you gotta go and force him to return to a place he didn't want to be.

I also didn't want my son to feel rejected—any more than he already had been by the undeserving Vivian. Especially not by me, his biological mother, who had missed out on raising him the past fifteen years. How would that be fair to me or to him?

We made small talk as we waited for Vivian to show up. She was five minutes late so far, and I started to wonder if she was like her mother—always showing up to planned events on her own time rather than the time agreed upon.

I checked my phone again and saw that she was now twenty minutes late.

"I'm going to give her a quick call and see if she's on her way," the woman said with a polite smile.

She placed the phone on speaker, and I heard it ring several times before rolling over to voicemail.

With Vivian clearly not showing up to the meeting, I was clueless as to what to do about his very false—but very real—runaway status.

"Can you talk to the police and tell them he's not a runaway, and that a meeting was set up and Vivian knows exactly where he is?" I asked.

"Our goal today was to help facilitate a meeting between the two of you in hopes you could come to an agreement for the sake of Jayshawn."

She looked at Jayshawn, and I could see pity on her face.

She was right to pity him. The life he once knew was over. He would never be able to go back to whatever his normal was—the way things were before he learned he was adopted, and before he realized she had lied all these years about being his mother. He would never be able to erase the pain of that same woman dropping him off.

"We don't advise the police… well, at least not in the way you're asking."

So no one could help me navigate this situation. I was on my own.

We used the remaining time speaking with the school counselor about how many of Jayshawn's classes he had begun missing. I was shocked by this, but I didn't let my face give it away. I had been waking up early and taking him to school. If he was missing classes, it was because he just wasn't walking to them.

I didn't blame him, though. When I was pregnant with him and going through a hard time with all the changes in my life, I couldn't focus on school either—nor had I even wanted to try.

"Let's grab something to eat," I said to Jayshawn as we exited the school counselor's office. "Crazy Vivian just never showed up or answered her phone."

"Probably couldn't get off work," Jayshawn replied, getting into the car.

"I mean, maybe—but she reported you as a runaway. You'd think she'd show up just to see you."

Jayshawn remained silent at that, and I felt bad for him. He must have been so torn—wanting to get to know me and bond, while also not wanting to be rejected by the woman he had called 'mother' for so long.

***

The knock at my door startled me. I was in the middle of switching laundry from the washer to the dryer. When I opened it, I saw Jayshawn, looking utterly exhausted.

The entire situation made no sense. Vivian going out of her way to try and stop me and Jayshawn from spending time together had clearly taken a toll on him mentally.

"You wanna read what my mom said?" he asked, holding up the phone I had lent him.

"Sure," I said, bracing myself as he handed me the phone. I tried not to cringe at the word mom in reference to Vivian—who was anything but.

Jayshawn: Do u want me to come home?

Vivian: Yes. And bring all my shit back, or you can just get picked up by Phx PD.

Jayshawn: You don't even want me no more. I heard you talking to Tashia. I was up the whole time, just pretending to be asleep.

Vivian: Jayshawn, I will always want you.

Vivian: Where are you at, Jayshawn?

Vivian: Are you coming to your niece's birthday party? U know she wants to see you.

Vivian: WYA, Jayshawn? I don't want to have to involve the police, but now that you've been gone more than 24 hours, they're gonna report you missing and do an AMBER Alert on all those addresses and license plates. So if you want to take it there I will just have to do that.

Jayshawn: I'm not missing…and I'll visit my niece soon.

Vivian: Where are you now? Me and my police escort are on the way to Glendale.

Jayshawn: Why you wanna know where I'm at?

Vivian: To pick you up. What do you think? You're coming home, so we're on our way.

Jayshawn: Your still my mom but I dont wanna live there. You were literally just gonna let me live with Tashia. and I am not in Glendale no more. I am back in Mesa at my girlfriend Angelica's

Vivian: No I was Not so you need to stop your bullshit and if u wanna go anywhere it would be wit you DAD so until i see u face to face ur missing and the police are looking for you wit me so i guess u wanna run but thats stupid

Vivian: Where do she live then?

Jayshawn: I will still go to school….and I don't know her address

Vivian: It's okay. We will check with the school and they will give police her address.

Jayshawn: Oh I am definitely not going home now. Y'all are taking it to far. You shouldn't have never dropped me off and grandmother shouldn't have brought her into my life.

Vivian: Thats fine. now that you saying that i can show the police u a run away so

Jayshawn: Thats not my house remember. I don't pay bills. and don't forget I broke into YOUR house.

Vivian: Its ok. where is my stuff and my key?? because I already pressed charges for breaking an entering and I'm going to get a restraining order on them Monday.

Jayshawn: Leaving Mesa now.

So bet they wont find me.

Vivian: Do what u think but I'm ur mom and I love u. U know that BUT me and the police will find u.

Jayshawn: And whats yours? My phone? My playstation?

Vivian: U can take my TV n house keys to ur grandmother's and leave it wit ur uncle or at her front door n I won't involve the police but if u can't do that then ima continue to have them goin to ppl house n lookn for u this is my last attempt to be koo about this so u make the decision and I just got Johnny address so I will give tht to if u wanna run run it up to u now. When I check Wit ur grandmother or uncle Curtis to see if u brought my stuff then I will stop trippn but u have til 6pm thts it!!!!

"Wow," I said after reading the thread. "One minute she's telling you to come home, and the next, she's telling you to take her TV to your grandmother's house."

"Yeah," Jayshawn muttered, his head down. His emotions were hard to read, but I could tell he was holding a lot in.

"She's a mess," I said, handing the phone back to him. "You okay?"

He nodded, but I knew better. The betrayal was fresh and raw, and I hated that Vivian had the power to hurt him like this.

As Jayshawn sank into the couch, I decided to let him have some quiet. He'd had a long day, and this entire situation with Vivian was weighing on him more than he was letting on. I headed back to the laundry room and finished folding clothes, giving him space to process everything.

My mind spun as I folded. Vivian's manipulations, her lies, the audacity of involving the police—it was all too much. But what hurt the most was seeing the toll it was taking on Jayshawn. He deserved peace, stability, and a home where he felt safe and loved.

I grabbed the last shirt from the pile and sighed deeply. I had done everything I could to ensure Jayshawn knew he was wanted and cared for, but it was clear this fight wasn't over. Vivian wasn't just going to let him go without a fight.

I walked back into the living room, where Jayshawn was staring blankly at his phone. "Hey," I said gently, "you want to grab some food? We can get take-out and just relax tonight."

Restraining Order

I had a long night at Destiny's house, hanging out with Jayshawn and TJ, watching them play Fortnite on the PlayStation. Now I was in a rush to get out the door. I snatched my keys off the hook by the front door and clicked the unlock button on my key fob as I walked to the car. I opened the trunk and started dragging my open house signs to load them in two at a time.

Out of the corner of my eye, I saw a man approaching. I lived off a busy street near a major intersection, so he could have just been crossing the road. Still, I kept an eye on him as I continued loading the car.

"Nicole?" the man called out just as I closed the trunk, now full of open house signs.

I turned to face him, startled to find him standing on my property, just an arm's length away.

"Yes?" I replied, wondering who he was and how he knew my name.

"You've been served," he said, handing me a manila envelope he must've been hiding behind his back. I took the envelope cautiously, watching as he walked back down my driveway toward his car without another word.

Confused, I climbed into the driver's seat and ripped open the envelope. Bold words at the top caught my attention immediately:

Injunction Against Harassment

My eyes scanned the page, stopping on Vivian's name listed as the plaintiff and my own name below as the defendant, along with a full physical description of me:

Black female, brown eyes, black hair. 5'5, 130 lbs.

So that was why she didn't show up at the school meeting. She was at the courthouse, filing a restraining order against me. Even now, after everything had come to light, she still refused to honor the agreement we'd made when I was pregnant. If she had her way—and she just might at this rate—I wouldn't be in Jayshawn's life at all.

I sat frozen in my driveway, knowing I was going to be late to my open house, but I kept reading.

Defendant/Plaintiff Relationship: This person is the birth mother of my adopted son.

This person? That was all I was to her? As if we didn't know each other in real life?

At least now she was finally admitting I was Jayshawn's biological mother instead of retelling some wild birthing story.

I kept reading, my rage building with every word.

Nicole has been sneaking around with my son, taking him both out of the county and the state without my permission. As far as I know, she has taken him to Tucson and Vegas. She has been allowing him to spend the night at her place and encouraging him not to return home. She actually picked him up from school and broke into my home to remove his possessions.

"This bitch!" I slammed my hands on the steering wheel, the horn blaring repeatedly. I had done most of what she described in her report, and I knew it was wrong. I just hoped it would go unchecked. But Vivian was always one step ahead, doing things I never saw coming. I was playing checkers while she was playing chess.

The runaway charges? A lie, but clever.

The restraining order? A response to me involving Child Protective Services. Another calculated move.

Clever.

Nothing I did was working in my favor, and this made me angry.

Why was the universe allowing me to constantly keep losing to Vivian?

I was barely focusing on the road as I drove. Two cars had already honked at me, warning me I was swerving into their lane. In my agitated state, I knew I shouldn't have been driving at all. I should have told the listing agent about the short notice cancellation and said I had a family emergency—and I would have, if I didn't hate not following through with my commitments.

It was a miracle I made it to the open house without hitting someone. I walked around the side of the house in search of the electronic lockbox. The clunky blue box was attached to the hose, and I knelt down, using my phone's Bluetooth to wirelessly open the box and retrieve the key.

The home I was at was a patio home located in Sun Lakes, a 55 and up community—meaning I was going to have a busy day full of people who already lived in the neighborhood coming to check out the home as an outing, rather than people looking to actually purchase. And I was not in the mood to entertain them today in the hopes that they would share my name and number with friends and family members who might actually be wanting to purchase.

With the day I had, I needed to unwind. I decided to skip going over to Destiny's house, given the restraining order I now had. Mendel was going to be working late, so a glass of wine, warm bath, and early bedtime it was.

I opened the front door, dragging the open house signs in behind me, when I was greeted by Jayshawn.

"Hey, what are you doing here?"

"Just needed some quiet."

"Destiny didn't tell you about the restraining order?" I asked, shocked to see him but also not about to ask him to leave. He had yet to return to his home with Vivian, and I could only imagine how loud Destiny's house must have been at any given hour.

"Yeah, she told me. That's crazy."

"This entire thing is crazy," I said, setting the open house signs by the door against the wall. I headed toward the kitchen. Jayshawn being here was not going to deter my plans of having some Moscato and a hot bath to wash all the stress from the day away.

I lit a scented candle and soaked in the bath, sipping my wine. By the time I was dressed and out of the bath, I went to check on Jayshawn. I found him sprawled out across the bed in the spare bedroom, mouth partly open, snoring.

I guessed we both had a tiresome day.

I closed the door and headed back to my bedroom on the other side of the house. I called Mendel to tell him I was going to sleep and to try not to wake me up when he got home.

Bang.

Bang, bang, bang.

I woke from my sleep. Someone was pounding hard on the door. I stayed in bed, not moving. Mendel wasn't home yet, and I was not prepared to deal with an angry Vivian looking for a fight again.

"Phoenix PD." I heard when the knocking stopped—and then it started up again.

I was wide awake now, fear pulsing through me. I couldn't open the door for the police. Jayshawn was asleep in my spare bedroom.

I rushed out of my room, down the hall past the living room and kitchen to the other side of the house where my son was sleeping. I turned on the light.

"Jayshawn!" I said in a distressed, loud whisper. The light had no effect on his sleep. He didn't even budge. "Jayshawn," I tried again, slightly louder.

Nothing.

I needed him to get up and hide in the backyard shed or alley like he did the last time cops came looking for him when he had been first reported as a runaway.

I shook his leg.

How was he still asleep?

Bang, bang, bang.

"Phoenix PD, we need to speak with you!"

Shit. Dammit.

"Coming!" I shouted.

I pulled the blanket Jayshawn had tangled around his legs and straightened it out before placing it back over him in a poor attempt to hide him.

I turned off the bedroom light and closed the door.

I opened the front door a crack and was immediately met with an officer inches from my face.

"Ms. Hayes."

"Yes," I said, completely terrified. I couldn't stop my body from shaking, and I just knew I was about to go to jail. Not juvenile detention. Jail. With adults.

"A Vivian has reported her son Jayshawn as a runaway and believes he is with you," the officer said. There were two police officers.

"Can we come in?" the first officer asked.

"I can come out." I pulled the door open just enough for my body to fit through it and closed it behind me. I knew I looked guilty as sin but couldn't let them in my home.

"Is he here with you?" the second officer asked.

"No," I said, lying through my teeth. My body was shaking so badly at this point.

"Are you alright?" the second officer asked, eyeing me.

"I'm just so cold. You guys woke me up out of bed." It was a half-lie this time, but my tone wasn't convincing, and I knew it. My nervous system was too shot. I couldn't even pull myself together if I wanted to.

"Do you have any idea where he's at?" he asked, and from his tone, I sensed he knew I was lying. He would have had to be the worst officer in history not to know.

More questions, but at least they weren't pushing to come into the house.

"At his friend's house."

"Which friend?"

This shit again.

"TJ," I said. These cops weren't voices over the phone I could simply hang up on. I had to answer their questions because upsetting them would not have a favorable outcome.

***

I was dialing Destiny's number the minute the door closed, and it only took a couple of rings before she picked up.

"Destiny. Tell me why Vivian reported Jayshawn as a runaway and the cops were just here."

"I know," she said, cutting me off. "The cops were just here too."

"What? They literally just left my house looking for him. Destiny! I could not fucking stop shaking the entire time they were questioning me. Thank God they didn't push to come in. Fucking Jayshawn sleeps like the dead."

"Damn. Well, I fucking told Glendale PD to come in and have a look around. Seriously."

"Yep. Told them to check the closets and under the beds."

Shit. They wouldn't have had to check under the bed over here.

"Yeah, that's crazy."

"You don't even know the stress I was feeling. Omg, I need a drink."

Return to Sender

My phone dinged, and I grabbed it, opening up a message from a 480 number.

"As you know, Jayshawn did not go home, but we still need to have the meeting at 10 a.m. Friday."

Anger flared up inside me as I typed out my response.

"Well, I told you yesterday he didn't want to go, but instead of advocating for him—for children like I believed you would when I called—you're threatening him with arrest. This fear is exactly what's keeping him away."

I knew what I was saying wasn't entirely true, but I kept going. I needed her to believe me, to feel guilty. She didn't need to know that I thought of CPS as little more than legal kidnappers who sometimes removed children from loving environments. In this case, though, I didn't believe Vivian's home was loving or caring at all. She clearly didn't want to care for Jayshawn, and the fact that they wouldn't let me—the woman who birthed him—care for him was beyond infuriating.

"You guys are simply trying to force him back to a home where he doesn't feel wanted anymore. Either way, I'm at work. I've contacted a lawyer, like I said I would, and I plan on reaching out to the Defender's of Children organization since calling you was clearly a mistake. You're not advocating for him."

Another lie. I hadn't contacted any such organization, nor did I even have a number for them. But my threat worked because I saw the three dots indicating Bianca was typing a response.

"DCS can't keep children from going home when there is no abuse going on," she texted back. Shortly after, another message arrived.

"No one threatened him. It is simply a fact that he could be arrested because he is considered a runaway and truant for not going to school."

Getting Jayshawn to school with a restraining order in place while driving a very noticeable bright yellow Jeep was no longer possible. Vivian had already notified the school about the restraining order and his runaway status. Just yesterday, they'd approached me in the parking lot and asked me to leave.

***

"I spoke with the Mesa police," Mendel said, his tone hesitant.

I cut him off before he could finish. "You did what?" My voice was sharp. "Why?"

"Just listen a second."

Frustrated, I took a deep breath and glared at him, waiting for him to explain.

"They said I can meet them at the QuikTrip gas station in Mesa, and they'll take him to Vivian's."

"Mendel, Jayshawn doesn't want to go back! He's told me since the moment he found out she wasn't his biological mother that he no longer wants to live with her. He wants to live with me!" I jabbed a finger into my chest. "Me! I'm his actual mother!"

"Nicole," he said, using my name like he was about to deliver some obvious truth. "You can't take him to school. You can't enroll him in a school near our house. The police think he's a runaway and won't stop looking for him. They've been coming to the house almost daily. And let's not forget your restraining order."

His points were valid, but it didn't make this any easier. "I don't want to just abandon him! Just hand him back to Vivian like he's some kind of unwanted puppy."

"If they find you with Jayshawn, Nicole, they'll arrest you. He can't live with you if you're in jail. Let's let Mesa PD take him back home, and then we can figure something out later. Go to the courthouse and ask for custody."

"You think I can just waltz into a courthouse and ask for custody?" I scoffed. "Mendel, I tried that already. Remember? Twelve years ago?"

"Listen," he said, his tone calm. "The police said once they have him, they'll remove him from the missing person and runaway list. Let's at least do that. Do you want to risk canceling our wedding because you're in jail?"

I exhaled sharply, realizing I didn't have much of a choice. "Fine. But you're going to have to tell him."

I followed Mendel into the spare room where Jayshawn was lying on the bed, playing a game on his phone while listening to music.

"I know this isn't what you want," Mendel began, sitting down next to him. "It's not what any of us want. But this situation with your mother and your adoptive mother has gotten really complicated. She's got a lot to lose, Jayshawn. The restraining order puts Nicole's real estate license in jeopardy. And if the police find you with her, she could go to jail and you could end up in Juvie."

"Okay," Jayshawn said quietly, his face reflecting sadness and defeat. It was a feeling I knew all too well.

"Do you want me to pack some of your things?" I asked, my voice soft.

"No, it's okay," he replied.

Jayshawn and Mendel left in Mendel's work van. I walked them to the door and gave Jayshawn a hug, hoping it conveyed how sorry I was.

I watched them drive off. After a few minutes of standing in the doorway, the cold air snapped me out of my daze. I closed the door and sat on the couch, but I couldn't stay still. I got up, opened the fridge, and stared blankly at its contents. Finding nothing appealing, I closed it and glanced at the clock on the stove. It had only been eight minutes since they left.

I picked up my phone and called Destiny.

"Mendel and I decided it's best that Jayshawn go back to Vivian's house," I told her. "At least this way, he won't be labeled as a runaway anymore."

"No, you guys did not!" she exclaimed, disbelief thick in her voice.

"Destiny, we had to. You know the board of realtors will revoke my license if this escalates further."

"I don't know about all that," she said dismissively, "but he's your son. He wants to live with you, not that liar Vivian."

"I know," I said, my voice barely above a whisper. "Let me call you back."

I hung up and immediately called Mendel.

"Hey."

"Hey. Are you there yet?"

"No, we stopped for food."

I let out a sigh of relief. "Tell him to forget it. Bring him back."

"Nicole, we already talked about this. Besides, I'm pulling into the QuikTrip now."

"Fine. Stay on the phone with me when you talk to the police."

"Nicole, I can't walk up to the police holding a phone. I'll call you after."

"Please," I begged. "Just keep the phone on speaker."

"I'm parking now," he said.

"Okay. Pocket, okay."

I could hear voices, but I couldn't make out what they were saying. I turned my phone volume all the way up. It didn't help. I hung up the phone and immediately called back. The phone went straight to voicemail.

He declined my call. Rude.

I sent Mendel a text message. "What is the police saying? Are they asking where he was or if he was with me?"

Four minutes passed before I saw my phone ding and light up, notifying me I had an unread message.

I opened it. "No, cops was cool."

Forget texting. I called Mendel again. "So everything went smoothly. You're on your way back or what?"

"Not yet."

"Why. What's happening?"

"The police officer is trying to get ahold of Vivian. I guess she isn't answering the phone."

"Oh. I thought they would just drive him to his house and drop him off."

"Yeah. I think they just wanted to notify her first, man. He is getting in the back of the cop car now."

"Did they handcuff him?"

"No. I be home in 30."

"You're leaving already?"

"What do you mean already? He is with the police. I am heading home."

"Okay."

***

When Mendel returned home, I couldn't help myself. I sent Jayshawn a message on social media.

"How's everything going? You okay?"

His reply came quickly:

"My mom's not answering, so I'm getting sent to DCS. Can't go anywhere until they get in touch with her. See, I shouldn't have come."

I typed back, my heart sinking:

"Yeah, we fucked up. I'm so sorry. Fuck, I blame Mendel."

I stared at my phone waiting for a reply, but no reply came.

Spring Break

MY sleep was restless, knowing that Jayshawn was currently sitting in a shelter—and it was my fault. I knew, without a doubt, that Vivian was punishing him for reaching out to me, for getting to know me, and for actually liking me. For learning that her lies about me weren't true. She had created an entire web of deception to keep him from wanting a relationship with me, and now she couldn't handle the fact that it didn't work.

I was forced to play this utterly ridiculous game, but I wasn't going to give up. Letting him go had been a mistake—one I'd already made twice. I wouldn't do it again. And now that he was in a shelter, I felt like I should be given custody automatically. If DCS couldn't reinstate my parental rights, I'd find out who could. In the meantime, I needed answers from Bianca.

I'd already left five voicemails on her phone and two with her supervisor. When she didn't call back, I decided to send a text.

"Did you reach her?" I wrote. She knew why I was calling, and the fact that she'd been ignoring me had my nerves on edge.

After a few minutes, her response finally came through: "I'm working on another case. I have spoken with his father, and he has a plan for Jayshawn. I'm sorry, but I cannot discuss it with you. He will be safe."

Why can't you talk to me about it? I fired back. Why should he sit in a shelter?

Her response was sharp: "For one, the restraining order. And two, you're not his legal parent."

I stared at the screen, fuming, but didn't bother replying. She was right—I did have a restraining order, and I hadn't been able to get it removed. When I'd gone to court to explain that I wasn't a threat to Vivian or my son, the judge ruled in her favor, upholding the order. He said my rights had been severed and that I was interfering with her ability to parent.

I texted Jayshawn on the phone I had recently purchased for him after Vivian destroyed the old work phone I'd given him.

What's going on, Jayshawn? Are you still at the shelter? I typed, holding my breath as I waited for his reply.

Yes, I'm still at the shelter, but they've been in touch with my father. His cousin in South Phoenix is going to come get me.

Oh wow. Have you not spoken with Vivian?

Nah, she still isn't answering.

Once your father signs the authorization form, will you be staying at his cousin's house?

Yeah, with Point. In South Phoenix.

***

Jayshawn spent a couple of nights at Point's house unhappily. He had been sleeping on the floor because there wasn't any space for him in the one-bedroom apartment. The place was old, the carpet was brown, and he hated it.

On the third day, he called Mendel and asked him to pick him up and take him back to Destiny's house.

At Destiny's, Jayshawn was contacted by both his dad and Vivian. Eventually, he took the light rail back to Mesa and returned home. Once there, he found himself unhappy with his living situation, sensing that Vivian didn't truly want him there anymore. The fridge was nearly empty, with only condiments and a half-full bottle of orange juice. Hungry, he sent me a picture of the barren shelves.

"I'm so sorry, Jayshawn," I texted back. "There's no way I can come to Vivian's house, but I can bring you some food and money if you can meet me at the apartment complex behind your house."

I knew I should have been avoiding contact with him, considering the restraining order, but I just couldn't do it. I kept calling to check on him, kept showing up when he asked. The restraining order was a hindrance, but it wasn't keeping me away from my son the way Vivian intended.

Jayshawn even attended my wedding to Mendel, and Vivian and Vanity were none the wiser. To be cautious, I made sure he wasn't in any of the photos, though in hindsight, I doubted either of them was paying close attention to his whereabouts. Vivian still wasn't doing anything differently in terms of his care. He came and went as he pleased, spending nights at Destiny's house whenever he wanted.

Feeling more confident that Vivian wasn't keeping tabs on him, I didn't think twice about bringing both Jayshawn and his best friend TJ along with me and Charlie for a spring break trip to Las Vegas.

We packed into my bright yellow Jeep: me, Jayshawn in the front seat playing DJ, and Charlie and TJ in the back. Mendel stayed back to work, of course. The ride to Vegas was smooth. Along the way, we saw another yellow Jeep Renegade, which was exciting, and had a bit of a race—until I had to stop for gas, ending the playful game between us.

We arrived in Vegas before dawn, just in time to stop at the iconic "Welcome to Las Vegas" sign. There was no parking nearby, so we parked farther back and walked. The boys complained, but I didn't mind; I needed to stretch my legs after the long drive.

TJ and Charlie had never been to Vegas, and though Jayshawn had been there once with Vivian on a family trip to Circus Circus, he didn't seem particularly impressed. I didn't ask too many questions about his trip with Vivian—I didn't want to hear about her.

After taking some photos, we headed to our Wyndham resort. It was slightly off the Strip but free thanks to points. The one-bedroom suite wasn't as large as I'd hoped. I took the bedroom and left the boys to sort out sleeping arrangements on the pullout couch.

Not long after, I heard yelling and a loud thud. I rushed out of the bedroom to find Jayshawn dragging Charlie off the bed while TJ stood awkwardly nearby.

"Let him go!" I demanded. "What the hell is going on?"

Charlie sat on the floor, holding his side. "You gave him rug burn," I said, annoyed.

"I'm tryna tell Charlie me and TJ sleeping on the bed and Charlie he in the room with you," Jayshawn said. "Me and TJ called it first. He just gon hop on the bed anyway like he ain't hear me."

I rolled my eyes. Charlie already had his reservations about Jayshawn, with him seeming to come out of nowhere. The restraining order didn't help, and Charlie had urged me not to spend time with him for fear of me getting arrested. On top of that, my two sons couldn't have been more different. They were four years apart, which was already a major difference, but then Jayshawn was into the culture—smoking weed, chasing girls, guns, rap, fast cars, jewelry, and luxury items, with money being especially important to him. Charlie was academic, read anime, would rather spend his time playing Monster Hunter or Dungeons & Dragons, and dreamed of becoming a zoologist. Jayshawn had dismissed Charlie as soft and nerdy, and Charlie labeled Jayshawn a common thug. Getting them to bond over something for real was going to be an uphill battle.

"Charlie, just come sleep in the room with me," I sighed.

***

Once I unpacked and had all my items where I wanted them, I went back to the living room. "Let's get food and explore."

We went for pizza and then walked in and out of hotels on the Strip, with Jayshawn and TJ stopping into a jewelry store.

"Can I see this?" Jayshawn asked a woman working behind the jewelry counter.

"Yes, of course," she said politely, and I wondered if she could tell he was just a 15-year-old kid with no money.

"He can't afford that," I said to the woman, not wanting her to think she might have a sale.

"But one day he might," she replied, smiling with encouragement—and that made both Jayshawn and TJ smile.

It made me loosen up and relax a bit. Typically, I didn't bother entertaining ideas or things I knew weren't within reach. But I guess the woman was right. I didn't know either of their futures. Maybe one day they could afford those items—or at least strive to—with hard work and determination. Who was I to rain on their window-shopping parade?

When we went into the next overpriced luxury store, I didn't say anything. I just let them look and take pictures while Charlie and I sat at an oxygen bar nearby.

"Did y'all really just spend $20 on air?" Jayshawn asked, as he and TJ approached the kiosk where Charlie and I were sitting, utterly shocked.

"It's not just oxygen. It's flavored. Want to try it?"

"Nah," Jayshawn said in a tone that suggested I couldn't have asked a stupider question.

"Well, let's get back to the resort. We'll find some fun stuff to do tomorrow."

Jayshawn had told me so much about Circus Circus that I decided we should go there for a bit. On the way in, I saw there was a massage spa nearby and decided to get one—plus, I kept losing track of everyone anyway, so I finally gave up trying to keep tabs.

"Going next door to get a massage," I typed into my phone and sent the message to both Charlie and Jayshawn.

By the time my massage was over, I was able to locate Jayshawn, TJ, and Charlie, and we headed out in search of food before finding something else to do.

Somehow, we convinced ourselves we were excited and willing to go bungee jumping—until we watched a few people go ahead of us. We realized just how high the drop was and completely changed our minds, happy instead to be spectators.

The next day I woke up, and we decided what we wanted to do. Vegas isn't really a place for kids—especially not kids who weren't really kids anymore. They were all in that in-between stage, which made them hard to please. I decided Fremont Street might be a win.

Stores, food, attractions, performers—both fully clothed and barely clothed—and people. So many people. With everyone on board, we piled into the car and headed to Fremont Street.

There was a crowd gathering, so we walked over to see what the fuss was about. A guy was hanging from a pull-up bar with a large timer behind him. "How long can you hang?" was written on a banner, along with "Beat the high score."

"Y'all should try this," I said to the boys.

"Shit, I know I can hang for a long time," TJ said, and I stared at him, unconvinced. He was a tall, lanky kid like Charlie. If he had muscles, I hadn't seen them. Maybe that would work in his favor.

They all got a turn and put up a good show—even Charlie, though he struggled to get up to the bar.

We bought some souvenir shirts and then headed to a zipline.

We took the elevator up 20 stories and snapped pictures on the landing. I realized I hadn't been taking any photos and wanted to have some for the trip.

Twenty stories up, it was freezing and windy. Normally, cold weather irritated me and triggered my asthma, but I was okay. We had bought jackets that said Vegas on them, and I put mine on. Charlie and I went on the zipline first, and I tried not to focus on falling to my death. It was a thrill for sure—especially with the frigid air and my intrusive thoughts reminding me that if I fell, I'd die plummeting between two tall buildings. Basically, an alleyway. Ugh.

I smiled and laughed my way through the ride, and right before Charlie and I reached the end, it snapped our picture.

Next up were Jayshawn and TJ, but Jayshawn couldn't be talked into getting on the ride, no matter what was said. And a lot was said. Charlie tried: "He's younger than you," "It's fun," "It's not that bad"—a whole series of arguments, all falling on deaf ears.

That left me going again, this time with TJ, who didn't want to ride alone. So once more, I risked my life, full of energy and excitement, as I zipped through the air 20 stories up.

The next morning, I woke up early to pack up and get out of the resort room by the 10 a.m. deadline.

I drove the long way home so we could stop at the Hoover Dam. We got lunch, took more pictures, and then hit the road again.

Once back in Arizona, I turned on my GPS and headed to Destiny's house to drop off both Jayshawn and TJ. Then Charlie and I headed home to enjoy the rest of the week before he had to catch a flight and return to his dad.

***

"Alright, Charlie," I said, giving him a big squeeze as his boarding group was called. "See you for your birthday in May."

"Okay." Charlie wasn't good at goodbyes, and frankly, neither was I.

"You've got to tell me what you want to do," I said.

"I don't know."

"I'll think of something. Love you."

"Love you too," he said, walking off without even looking back.

I hated goodbyes so much that I couldn't find my car. My mind was so distraught I couldn't think straight. I had been walking around the airport parking garage for what felt like an hour, and I was about to lose my mind.

Maybe this was just everything crashing down on me. Long-lost son. Restraining order. Second son, wanting all my attention—and maybe not so happy to have a brother. That same son living with his father, with me only seeing him five times a year. Recently getting married. And now finding out I was pregnant. For the third time.

I tried to think about what looked familiar to me, but nothing did. I knew I had turned in at four, so my car had to be somewhere on Level 4. I thought I'd parked near the elevators, but at this point, I couldn't be sure of anything.

I called Mendel, and his phone rang three times before he finally picked up.

"I can't find where I parked."

"Your car is yellow. You don't see it?" he asked, and I let out a tired laugh.

"No. I've literally been walking around for an hour looking for it."

"Are you on the right side? Maybe you parked on the other side."

"There's another side?"

"Yeah. Go back inside and walk to the other side. That's probably where you parked."

"Lord. I am so damn tired."

"Okay, call me back when you find it. Got to go."

I was even sad that he wanted to hang up so soon when I was this over-whelmed—but I figured a lockout call must have come in.

I walked across to the other side of the airport and into the parking garage—and sure enough, there was my bright yellow Jeep. Level 4. Exactly where I thought I'd parked.

Caught in the Act

The last 30 days had been an emotional roller coaster of indecision. Spend time with Jayshawn. Don't spend time with him. Keep my distance and only speak over the phone. Or, obey the law and cut contact completely. With Passover just days away, I was preparing for a flight to Michigan. My husband's entire family lived back East: Pittsburgh, New Haven, and Oak Park, Michigan. We would be spending the holiday in Oak Park.

"Hi, can I get two sausage egg McMuffins, two hash browns, and a large sweet tea?" I said into the speaker outside the McDonald's drive-through.

"Will that be all?" the woman's voice asked.

"Actually, let's add an order of hotcakes with a side of sausage and another large sweet tea." I decided I was hungry too.

I pulled up to the second window, grabbed my order, and set the bags on the passenger seat. Before driving off, I entered the address Jayshawn had texted me into my phone's GPS.

"I'm here," I texted him as I pulled into the small parking lot of his school. The school was a small alternative high school in a strip mall designed for students who needed to recover credits to graduate on time. With everything that had happened recently, Jayshawn had missed too much school and had been dropped by Westwood. This was his only option now if he wanted to complete schooling.

I considered parking in one of the parking spaces, unsure of how long it would take him to come out, but decided instead to circle the lot and just wait. On my second lap, I saw him exit the building.

I inched my car forward, passing cars parked to the left of me near the school entrance. Suddenly, I noticed a plump, dark-skinned woman in a silver car. Her jet-black hair and skinny, drawn-on eyebrows were hard to miss. I looked out my side mirror, trying to get a better look at the woman I had just passed. I felt a cold shiver as recognition hit me.

"It can't possibly be Vivian," I muttered aloud, glancing at Jayshawn as he approached my car.

"What?" he asked, but his focus was already on the McDonald's bag I'd brought him.

"You forgot the strawberry jelly," he said, unbothered.

I didn't respond. My attention was on the silver car pulling out of its parking spot. The woman inside raised her phone, pointing it directly at us.

Shit. Shit. Shit.

My eyes widened in shock.

"It's Vivian," I said, panic rising in my voice. Jayshawn froze mid-bite, finally grasping the gravity of the situation.

I put the car in drive. "I have to go," I said urgently.

He lingered, standing in the open car door, oblivious to the crisis unfolding. "Move!" I shouted.

The second he stepped back, I floored it. The door slammed shut from the force of my acceleration.

But it was too late. Vivian's car was right beside mine, her arm outstretched with her phone aimed at me. For one brief, gut-wrenching moment, our eyes met.

I turned out of the parking lot and onto the first side street I saw, heart pounding.

***

How in the hell was I going to spin this?

What reason could I possibly give for being there? Shopping? But why would I have been shopping in Mesa when I lived all the way in Phoenix? And the McDonald's bag? There was no way to explain the food.

I drove aimlessly, replaying the scene over and over in my mind. She definitely got a picture of my license plate. Even if she didn't get a clear shot of me, the strip mall had cameras everywhere.

I was screwed. Vivian had caught me red-handed.

I couldn't believe that after all these months of breaking the restraining order with Vivian none the wiser, this was how I got caught—bringing my son food.

And of course, Vivian called the police. I just knew she did. She didn't want Jayshawn, but she didn't want me to have him either. Her hatred for me made no sense. If she had kept her word all those years ago, we could have avoided this. But no—she had to lie, manipulate, and steal my son. She was the catalyst for everything that had gone wrong in my life. If I were a villain, she would have been my origin story.

I sat in my driveway, too nervous to go inside. Surely the police would show up at any moment to arrest me. I waited 10 minutes, then 20, then 45. When no flashing lights appeared, I finally went inside.

Even then, I couldn't relax. My nerves were frayed, and I couldn't shake the feeling that the police would come knocking any second. I called Destiny and vented about what had happened. After that, I called Mendel, warning him I might be in jail by the time he got back from his trip.

But as the day went on, no police showed up ready to drag me away in hand-cuffs. Maybe Vivian hadn't called the police after all.

For the next two weeks, I kept my distance. I didn't contact Jayshawn directly, instead getting updates from Destiny or Mendel. It was excruciating, but I couldn't risk pushing Vivian further.

Despite everything, I couldn't shake the guilt. Letting him go—again—was a mistake I wouldn't make a third time.

Consequences

I happened to be standing in my kitchen when I saw the mailwoman come up the walkway. I walked outside and checked the mail, finding it was mostly junk except for one manila envelope from the Mesa Municipal Court marked certified mail. My hands shook as I quickly tore the envelope open, knowing the words printed on the paper wouldn't reveal anything good. I was also a bit shocked it had taken them this long—it had been two months since the incident.

State of Arizona vs. Nicole Hayes

Domestic Violence

My eyes lingered on the words for a bit. Why did it say "domestic violence"? No one was hurt or harmed. Maybe they got something wrong, and I could get off on this technicality.

I kept reading.

The file number—who cared. Some other numbers at the top right—I skipped over, searching for the body of the document. Finally, I got to a part that was just words and no more numbers.

The undersigned complaint, pursuant to Arizona Rules of Criminal Procedure Rules 2.3, 2.4, and 3.1, complains and says upon information and belief:

That one Nicole Hayes, on or about April 18, 2019, in the city of Mesa, Maricopa County, Arizona, did commit a misdemeanor, to wit:

Interference with Judicial Proceedings: DV Offense.

Did knowingly disobey or resist a lawful order, process, or other mandate of a court. A Class 1 misdemeanor. A.R.S. 13-2810(A)(2). An offense involving domestic violence pursuant to A.R.S. 13-3601(A).

All of which is contrary to the statutes of Arizona in such cases made and provided, and against the peace and dignity of the city of Mesa and the state of Arizona.

Wherefore complainant prays that a summons be issued for said defendant and that he/she be dealt with as the law directs.

06/24/2019

"Well," I sighed out loud angrily. I knew this was coming. It was Vivian—of course, she had pressed charges. The Mesa Police Department just moved slow. So slow, in fact, that I had started to think maybe, because I fled the scene before they arrived, I hadn't truly been caught. I saw how ridiculous that thought was now. I wasn't sure why they didn't just come get me that day or the next, but they were summoning me now.

I turned the page and saw my charge listed again, along with another order.

The defendant is ordered to appear at The Mesa Municipal Court on or before August 26, 2019.

I called Mendel up and told him what the paper said—that Vivian did, in fact, pursue criminal charges against me, and I had to appear in court and get fingerprinted before or on August 26th.

"Should we look for a lawyer?" he asked.

I took a deep breath before responding. This entire situation was just so draining. My stomach hurt, and I felt as if I could throw up. I knew my nervous system was going through it. I was scared. I was angry. I was sad. I chose to grasp onto the strongest emotion I was feeling.

Anger.

Anger had been the emotion that had gotten me through so many hard times already, and it would have to be strong enough to get me through this as well.

"Well, we should probably speak to somebody. However, I don't know what good it will do," I replied.

"Why not?"

"Mendel!" I said, exasperated and taking my anger out on him. "I am guilty, and I was caught. Vivian literally saw me." I stressed the "saw me" part. We had locked eyes. She probably got a picture for all I knew, and because Jayshawn was so focused on eating, he didn't even move out of my way so I could drive off in time.

***

Deciding to live by the motto "Never put off until tomorrow what you can do today," I went to the courthouse for fingerprinting before August. I also wanted to request a copy of the police report while I was there because I needed to know what Vivian had even told the police.

"I'm looking for fingerprinting," I said to the woman sitting at the information desk just off the side of the security check-in.

"You're gonna make a left, and it's the second door. Just take a seat, and someone will check you in."

"Thanks. And where can I get a copy of the police report?"

"You'll pull a number over there." She pointed behind her. "And someone will call you."

"Okay." I thanked her once more and took a seat in front of a small room that could only be for fingerprinting. I waited to be called.

I dug around in my purse for my driver's license so that I was prepared when called and not fumbling around in my large tote bag.

"Nicole," I heard my name called by a man in uniform poking his head out of the small room. I stood up and started walking over but suddenly felt embarrassed. I felt like I should explain myself.

I was wearing a light pink maternity dress that hugged me tightly, accenting my growing baby bump, along with sandals with a low heel. I was married and finally had a child on the way that wasn't out of wedlock. I had made something of myself by obtaining not one degree but two—a bachelor's in communications and a master's in elementary education. But here I was, about to get my fingerprints taken like a common criminal.

For domestic violence, of all things.

I hated that that's the way the charges were categorized simply because we were related or familiar or whatever it was. It was bullshit, and I felt self-conscious.

As I nervously stood by the electronic fingerprinting machine, the policeman entered data into the computer.

"Give me your left hand," he commanded, barely looking to see that I had complied.

I raised my hand, and he grabbed my wrist, placing my entire left hand on the surface of the screen. He then placed my thumb down, followed by each of my fingers.

"Right hand."

I raised my right hand as well, and he placed it on the screen.

"I didn't hit anybody or anything," I started, feeling the need to defend myself.

"Relax your hand," the officer said, giving my wrist a little shake.

"I brought my son breakfast," I said as the officer continued to place each of my fingers on the screen. "How is that a crime?" I asked, which earned me a slight glance but no response. I realized I should probably stop talking. He didn't care, and I shouldn't be self-incriminating. This officer appeared bored and could probably care less whether I had committed the crime or not. His job was to fingerprint me, and that's what he was doing.

He finished and let my hand go. I instinctively wiped them on the sides of my dress. He printed out a paper that I took without looking at and exited the small room. The courthouse had gotten busy while I was in there. Long lines had formed, and the lobby was full of people sitting. I walked to the center of the room and pulled a number.

106.

I looked at the wall and saw that they were only on number 54. I took a seat.

My turn finally arrived 45 minutes later, and I was now sitting in the front seat of my car, staring down at the incident report. I had quickly skimmed it after receiving it, but now I was reading it line by line.

The bold word "Offender" followed by my name, social security number, height, weight, address, and a phone number that wasn't even mine. I wasn't sure whose number the officer had plugged in there. I scanned the time and date of the offense.

April 18, 2019, 9:41 AM and the physical address and location of the incident.

Offense: Failure to comply with court order – DV.

Under "Victim" I saw my son's name, with the word juvenile in parentheses. His personal information was redacted, which seemed pointless, but whatever. I turned to the next page.

Narrative: On 4-18-2019, at approximately 0941 hrs., I was dispatched to 822 S Alma School Rd (Food City) in reference to RP (reporting party), Vivian Alexander, reporting her 15-year-old son, Jayshawn Alexander, had run away from her in the parking lot. Vivian says she has an (OOP) order of protection against Jayshawn's birth mother, Nicole Hayes, and that Nicole was in the parking lot with Jayshawn. Her presence upset him, and he took off.

I lifted my eyes from the paper and went over what I had just read in my mind. It seemed as if she was telling the officer my presence upset Jayshawn and caused him to run away from her—or did I read it wrong?

Ugh. She was such a liar.

I went back to reading the report.

I made contact with Vivian while other officers were trying to locate Jayshawn. Vivian said that Jayshawn attends Pinnacle High School at 810 S Alma School in the same strip mall, just north of the Food City. Vivian said that she has an OOP with Jayshawn listed as another protected party against Nicole. Vivian says that she observed Nicole in the parking lot near the school giving Jayshawn food for lunch.

"It was breakfast, dummy," I said to my empty car.

Vivian said she approached them, and Jayshawn took off, and Nicole left in a yellow truck.

"It's a Jeep, and your fat ass never left your vehicle," I muttered.

Vivian said that no one else saw Nicole with Jayshawn.

"Maybe that's a good thing," I muttered, then read on.

I had MPD dispatcher M. Carlin confirm the OOP, which had been served to Nicole 01/16/2019. I obtained a copy of the OOP from Vivian, which listed herself and Jayshawn as protected and Nicole as the defendant.

Jayshawn was located behind the Food City by officers Counts and Helenius and brought back to the school. Vivian said she desired prosecution.

"Of course she did."

I had been unable to locate any witnesses who observed Nicole and Jayshawn. I had been unable to make contact with Nicole. Based on this report, I forwarded this to the DV Detectives to locate and interview Nicole.

There was another, longer report still, titled "Supplement Notes."

On April 22, 2019, I was assigned Mesa Department report 1080218 for follow-up.

I reviewed the officer's initial report for further details. On Thursday, April 18, 2019, officers responded to Food City located at 822 S. Alma School in Mesa, Arizona, in reference to an order of protection violation. Once on the scene, officers contacted the reporting party, Vivian. Vivian informed the officers she had an order of protection against suspect Nicole Hayes. She explained she had guardianship of Nicole's fifteen-year-old son, victim Jayshawn. Vivian informed officers Jayshawn attended Pinnacle High School, which was in the strip mall. Vivian stated she saw Nicole in the parking lot near the school giving the victim food. She said she approached them, and Jayshawn fled, and Nicole took off in her vehicle. Jayshawn was later found behind the Food City and brought back to school.

I stopped reading and dropped the report onto my lap. The lies and exaggerations were exhausting. I knew that no matter how much I read, the words would only confirm what I already knew: I messed up. And Vivian, as always, made sure I would pay for it.

On May 9, 2019, the report continued, the detective contacted the Maricopa County Sheriff's Office to confirm Superior Court Order #CV090642 was a valid court order. A copy of the court order was faxed to the Fiesta Substation and attached to the case.

"The order listed Vivian as the 'Plaintiff,' Jayshawn as the 'protected person,' and Nicole Hayes as the 'defendant.' The court order read: No Contact."

I skimmed over the rest of the paragraph, already knowing what it said. I knew exactly what I violated when I went to give Jayshawn food before my flight that day.

Due to Nicole residing in Phoenix, I attempted to contact her by telephone several times. I was unable to make any contact with Nicole or leave a message.

"Complete bullshit," I scoffed. Leave a message? Sir, you must not have called at all. I had this weird need to answer every call that came to my phone. Plus, I hated notifications piling up, so I always checked my voicemails. My voicemail box wouldn't have been so full that he couldn't leave a message. But whatever. This lie didn't change the trouble I'd gotten myself into this time.

On May 9, 2019, I contacted Jayshawn at Pinnacle Peak High School.

The detective described how he briefly spoke to Jayshawn outside, privately.

I introduced myself to him and explained I was following up on the incident. My conversation with Jayshawn was recorded and uploaded into VideOversight. The following was a summary of the recording for details: Jayshawn told me he was at school when he received a text message from Nicole.

Why did he always have to be so damn honest?

He said Nicole was moving out of state and was going to drop off his backpack that he had left at her house.

Moving? Why did everyone keep getting this wrong? I was going out of town—not moving. Geez.

Jayshawn said he responded back to Nicole's text, asking her to bring him McDonald's for lunch.

"It was breakfast!" I shouted at the paper. 9:41 a.m.! McDonald's didn't even serve lunch yet.

I questioned Jayshawn if he knew there was an order of protection prohibiting Nicole from contacting him, and he responded, "No."

Finally, a lie. But after spilling everything else, what was even the point?

I thanked him for talking to me and directed him back to class.

I continued to the next section of the document.

Due to the totality of this investigation, Vivian placed Nicole on the property talking to Jayshawn and Jayshawn placed Nicole at the incident location.

"Well thanks."

I believed there was probable cause to charge Nicole with violation of ARS 13-2810A2 Interfering with Judicial Proceedings -DV.

I submitted a long form complaint to the Mesa City Prosecutor's office for further review. Victims' rights were mailed to Jayshawn C/O Vivian. A criminal history check for Nicole was attached to this report. This concluded my involvement in this case.

I turned the page and saw my name once again at the top under defendant. I skimmed the charges, location, and probable cause. I turned the page, finding nothing of interest there. The next page was a questionnaire that had been filled in poorly, asking for additional information.

I scanned the words.

List any priors.

Arrest? FTA, Failure to show DL, Driving on Suspended, DUI, Resisting Arrest, Aggravated Assault, Escort.

Convicted? FTA, Failure to show DL, Driving on Suspended, DUI, Resisting Arrest, Aggravated Assault, Escort.

The aggravated assault shouldn't have been in my conviction categories. My sister had stolen my identity, and I was cleared. It should have said dismissed. So annoying. Actually, all of my charges were annoying.

FTA? Several

Oh geez. Writing several in that column was so unnecessary.

I hated having a criminal record.

The report droned on about Vivian's claims and the detective's conversations with Jayshawn. It was all a web of small inaccuracies and truths twisted just enough to make me look worse. But in the end, the facts didn't lie: I was there. I saw Jayshawn. I gave him food.

I threw the report onto the empty passenger seat and watched as it slid to the floor while I drove. This whole situation felt like such bullshit. I needed to do something familiar and comforting, something that would calm my nerves and take my mind off this disaster.

I pulled into a Dutch Bros drive-thru. The chirpy voice from the speaker startled me from my thoughts.

"Hey! How's your day going?" A young woman with a cheerful, Nickelodeon-sitcom energy greeted me.

"Great," I lied, mustering a smile.

I ordered my usual—a white chocolate chai tea with the works—and let her bubbly energy distract me from the reality of my situation. It worked, if only for a moment.

By the time I got back to the house, my tea was half gone, and I had rehearsed a million different excuses in my head for why I was at Jayshawn's school that day. None of them would save me, but they kept me from spiraling into panic.

Not Guilty

We parked in the garage, and Mendel and I quickly headed toward the courthouse entrance. I tried to keep my breathing steady, but my chest felt tight, the weight of what might happen bearing down on me with every step.

Inside, we passed through security, placing our belongings on the scanner. The sterile atmosphere of the courthouse only amplified my nerves. I checked the monitor for my name to find the courtroom where my hearing would take place.

We stepped into the elevator, and I tried to lighten the mood with a joke. "Well, Mendel, looks like we'll be spending our honeymoon apart—me in jail for six months to a year."

Mendel didn't laugh. Instead, he placed a reassuring hand on my shoulder. "You're not going to jail," he said, his tone calm and steady. I wanted to believe him, but his optimism felt distant, like a comforting blanket he could wrap himself in because he wasn't the one standing on the edge of a cliff.

Missing me while he was at home was one thing. Missing me while I was locked up? That was a reality only I might face.

The courtroom was sterile and cold, the kind of place that felt designed to drain any sense of hope. Mendel and I sat in the public seating area. I glanced around, taking in the faces of other defendants. Some looked defiant, others defeated. I tried to study the judge, but he was impossible to read. His responses were curt and matter-of-fact, giving no indication of whether he leaned toward leniency or severity.

The prosecutor was the only person in the room who seemed genuinely happy. Her professional detachment didn't soothe me—it only sharpened my anxiety.

When my name was called, a nervous energy flooded my body. My legs felt shaky as I made my way to the podium, my palms clammy as I gripped its edge.

The judge's voice was steady as he instructed me, "Please state your name for the record."

I swallowed hard and forced my voice to sound calm. "Nicole Hayes," I said, though I was anything but composed.

The judge began outlining the charges against me: a class one misdemeanor for violating a court order—a charge tied to domestic violence because of its legal classification.

My stomach churned as the prosecutor began to speak, outlining the evidence against me. "On or about April 18, Ms. Nicole Hayes was seen in her yellow Jeep outside the school of the protected party, Jayshawn."

Hearing it out loud felt like a punch to the gut. I knew I was guilty of everything she was saying, and my guilt was written all over my face. I cringed, but I couldn't do anything except stand there and listen.

"How do you plead to the charges?" the judge asked.

I hesitated. Saying "guilty" would have been honest, but it would also have sealed my fate. "Not guilty" felt like a lie, one that would eventually unravel. My mind raced.

"Hypothetically speaking," I began, my voice trembling as I glanced between the judge and the prosecutor, "if I violated the restraining order, it was only to give him food and money because his adoptive parent wasn't providing for him. Would that be a valid exception?"

The judge's expression didn't change. "Ms. Hayes," he said evenly, "neither I nor the prosecutor can advise you on how to plead. Have you spoken with a lawyer?"

"No," I admitted, my voice barely above a whisper.

"I strongly recommend you consult with a lawyer," the judge said firmly. "For now, we have court-appointed legal aid available to answer your questions."

I had already spoken to a lawyer when I first got the summons to go to court, and it hadn't seemed like there was much to be done in the case of violating a direct court order, so I hadn't bothered hiring him.

I was directed to a small room outside the courtroom. A legal aid attorney walked in shortly after, introducing herself as Stacey. She had a kind demeanor, which immediately caused my composure to crumble.

"It's just not fair," I said, my voice cracking as tears spilled down my cheeks. "This whole situation is so messed up. She doesn't even want him. Why is she making my life so miserable?"

Stacey slid a box of tissues across the table. I grabbed a few, wiping my face, smudging my makeup.

"I'm not a bad person," I continued, my voice breaking. "I just want to have a relationship with my son. I want to make sure he's cared for and has food. I don't deserve to go to jail."

Stacey listened patiently, but I knew she couldn't change the outcome of my case. Despite this, I kept talking, unloading my frustrations and fears until my sobs finally subsided.

"Do you need more time to find a lawyer?" Stacey asked gently.

"Yes," I replied, grasping for the only option that might buy me some time. "I need more time."

When I returned to the courtroom, it was well past noon. The judge looked as tired as I felt.

"I understand you've spoken with legal aid," he said.

"Yes," I confirmed.

"Are you ready to enter a plea, or are you seeking counsel from a lawyer?"

I thought a minute before choosing the only answer that would buy me the time I needed and keep me from having to enter a plea that day.

"A lawyer, Your Honor."

He nodded and set a new arraignment date for four weeks later. As I left the courtroom, Mendel was waiting for me, his hand warm and steady on my back as we walked out.

The thought of facing Vivian again made my stomach twist. I hadn't been ready the last time we were in court, and honestly, I wasn't sure I'd ever be ready.

My past experiences with the system should have prepared me, but nothing could fully brace me for the way it broke you down. I had shown up last time, ready to tell my side of the story, to explain the injustices I'd faced. But instead of being heard, I was cornered, my words drowned out by a system determined to label me as the villain.

The anxiety seeped into every corner of my life. It caused tension with Mendel. He was optimistic, believing I could explain myself and the judge would understand. He was convinced I'd find a way out of this, but I knew better. Things rarely went my way, even when I followed the rules. Now that I'd broken them, I couldn't imagine any mercy.

When I returned to court weeks later, I faced the same judge. This time, when asked how I pleaded, I said, "Not guilty."

I still didn't have a lawyer. I hadn't even tried to find one after my initial consultation left me disillusioned. Pleading not guilty felt risky. It meant a trial. It meant Vivian would testify against me. It meant I'd have to come up with a compelling reason for why I had been there in the first place—something more convincing than the truth.

The trial was set for another four weeks out. Four weeks to come up with something, anything, that might keep me out of jail. But as I left the courthouse, I had no plan, no answers—just a gnawing fear that time was running out.

Awaiting Trial

The weeks between court dates stretched out like a prison sentence of their own. Every morning, I woke up with a knot in my stomach, the weight of uncertainty pressing against my chest. Mendel did his best to keep me grounded, but his optimism often felt like it existed in a separate reality—one where things always worked out for the best. I wasn't living in that reality.

My days became a blur of routines that felt hollow. I kept up appearances, answered real estate calls with a chipper voice, met clients with forced smiles, and made small talk that felt both mundane and absurd. How could I pretend to care about square footage and backyard pools when the shadow of a trial loomed over everything? But I needed the distraction, however artificial it might have been.

Mendel, ever the steady hand, tried to fill the silence with light conversation at dinner. "You've got to stop spiraling," he said one evening, watching me push spaghetti around my plate. "You'll drive yourself crazy before the court date even arrives."

"I'm already crazy," I snapped, then softened, guilt washing over me. "I'm sorry. It's just… what if I really go to jail, Mendel? What then? What happens to you? To the baby?" My voice broke, and I stared down at my untouched food, willing the tears to stay back.

He reached across the table and took my hand. "It won't come to that," he said firmly. "We'll figure it out. You're not going to jail."

But he didn't have answers to the questions that kept me awake at night.

The nights were the hardest. Lying in bed, staring at the ceiling, I replayed every decision that had led me here. I kept circling back to that first message, the one that had set everything in motion.

Jayshawn was essentially homeless now, a casualty of Vivian's vendetta against me. He had no stable home, no consistent Wi-Fi for his online classes, and no one truly looking out for him.

I dialed back my contact with him in the weeks following the arraignment, afraid that even a stray phone call might give Vivian more ammunition against me. But the guilt of leaving him in limbo gnawed at me constantly. When we did talk, I treaded carefully, trying to nudge him toward convincing Vivian to drop the charges.

"Have you talked to her?" I asked one evening, my voice careful, almost casual.

"Not really," Jayshawn said. "She's been… Vivian. You know how she is." There was a heaviness in his voice that matched my own.

"Maybe… maybe you could talk to her," I ventured.

He laughed bitterly. "Yeah, because she's really gonna listen to me."

"I know," I sighed. "But it's worth a shot, right? Maybe she'll drop the charges." The words felt hollow even as I said them, but I had to try. What else could I do?

Jayshawn didn't answer. The silence stretched out between us until he finally muttered, "Shit, I guess I can see if she answers my call." It hadn't been much, but it was all I had to hold onto.

The days crawled by, each one bringing me closer to the trial. I kept Mendel updated on the case, though it felt like I was rehashing the same uncertainties over and over again.

"I still don't know what I'm going to say," I admitted one night as we lay in bed. "What if I freeze up? What if I say the wrong thing?"

"You'll be fine," Mendel said, his voice calm but tired. "Just tell the truth."

I stared at the ceiling, the weight of his words pressing down on me. "The truth is why I'm here," I whispered. "The truth is, I broke the law."

He didn't have an answer for that.

The only relief I found was in the brief moments of normalcy that managed to break through the tension. An unexpected laugh during a movie we watched together, the rhythmic comfort of folding laundry, even the mindless repetition of checking real estate listings. These small distractions were like breaths of fresh air in a room that was otherwise suffocating.

I also leaned heavily on my friends, called Destiny and Kaila more often than usual. They listened without judgment, offering advice that was equal parts practical and emotional.

"Just stay out of trouble until the trial," Destiny warned. "No more sneaking around with Jayshawn."

"I'm not sneaking around," I said defensively, though we both knew it wasn't entirely true.

Kaila was more pragmatic. "Get a lawyer, Nicole. A good one. Even if it costs you. This is your life we're talking about."

They were both right, of course, but neither of their advice eased the constant knot in my stomach.

As the trial date drew closer, the weight of uncertainty grew heavier. Every decision, every conversation, felt like it could tip the scales one way or the other. And through it all, I tried to prepare myself for the possibility I couldn't ignore—I might lose. I might go to jail.

The Big Day

I was awoken by a loud, relentless chirping. I rolled over, reaching for my phone on the nightstand.

It was 7:30.

I didn't have time to hit the snooze button that day. I hopped immediately out of bed and headed for the bathroom and turned on the hot water. It would only take a few minutes to heat, but I left the bathroom and headed for my closet to once again look for an outfit that would make me look less like a rule breaker and more like a law-abiding citizen.

"Mendel. Come on, get ready," I said, pulling out an outfit from my closet and setting it on the foot of my bed.

"Okay, okay. I'm getting up," Mendel said, hopping out of bed. "I'm gonna make a coffee and get ready soon."

I got out of the shower, dressed, and applied some makeup to my face. Ready to go, I stood by the door and called to Mendel.

Damn, I was so nervous. I really hoped I could talk my way out of this. Get the judge to understand—we had just gotten married, and I could go away for up to a year.

"That reminds me," Mendel said, pulling out his phone.

"What? Who are you calling? We have to go. We're gonna be late."

Mendel put up a finger, and I paused.

"Rabbi? Nicole has court today. Yeah, you know the drama with her son. She wants to give tzedakah. For a good omen," he said into the phone, and I rolled my eyes. Of course I wanted all the help I could get not to go to jail, but I had never been superstitious to the point of believing donating money to a religious establishment would affect an outcome relating to my life.

"We'll put $50 in the pushka."

His belief in a higher power had him believing tzedakah would help me.

I knew better.

There was no higher power clearing His schedule to help me.

"Yeah, okay. Say goodbye and come on," I said, holding the front door open.

***

I was in a good mood as I walked into the court building and went through the security line. For the past week, I had decided to stop worrying and take my husband's advice of just being positive. I had listened to upbeat, good-vibe music the entire 30-minute car ride.

After walking through the security checkpoint—which took no time at all—I looked for my name on the monitor to see what courtroom I needed to go to. I scanned the monitor for two minutes as it sat on one screen before flashing to another to show more names. My name wasn't on either screen for any of the 8:30 a.m. time slots.

"Mendel. I don't see what courtroom I'm in."

He scanned the monitor as well, making sure I hadn't missed anything.

"Yeah, that's weird."

"Should we just go up and check the court we were in last time? I'm sure it's the same judge."

I pressed the elevator button impatiently, even though I knew pressing it once versus five times wouldn't make the elevator open its doors any faster.

After what felt like 10 minutes—but was probably only one—the elevator opened up, and I repeatedly pressed the circle with the number 3 on it until the door closed and we were finally moving.

I exited the elevator with Mendel on my heels and headed straight for the courtroom I had been in three times so far since violating the bogus restraining order. The courtroom was the last room all the way at the end of the building. As Mendel and I speed-walked, we didn't pass a single person lingering in the halls near any of the courtrooms. The corridor was unusually quiet, and it made me wonder where all the people were. I could see out the window as we walked that there were a lot of cars parked in the parking lot, so why did the building seem so quiet?

I reached the courtroom door before Mendel and swung it open to find it completely empty.

"Well, this isn't the courtroom. It's empty," I said, stating the obvious.

"Are you sure this was the one?" Mendel questioned.

"I thought so, but maybe it's the one before," I said, closing the door.

We headed to the next courtroom, but it was locked. There was another room, and when I opened that, I saw what looked to be a meeting happening and quickly shut the door. There was only one more courtroom to check before we were back to the elevator. We got to that door, and it was locked as well.

"There's no way we got the floor wrong," I said, truly starting to doubt my memory.

"I don't know. We can stop on level two."

Getting back into the elevator, I pressed the circle with the number two on it and glanced at my phone for the time. It was almost 9 a.m. We had wasted 15 minutes looking for the courtroom and were now late.

When I stepped off the elevator this time, I saw plenty of people in the halls sitting on benches outside the courtrooms. I scanned the monitors mounted outside the courtrooms and still didn't see my name. I checked all the courtrooms before getting back into the elevator to head back to the main floor.

I walked over to the information desk that was stationed smack dab between the security and the elevators me and Mendel had just gotten off of.

There was a woman sitting behind the counter.

"I was supposed to have court today at 8:30," I said, seeing that it was now 9:06 a.m., "but I didn't see my name on the monitors anywhere, and I don't know which courtroom I'm supposed to be in," I said hurriedly.

"You're gonna have to pull a number and speak to someone at the window," she said, and I thought about how pulling a number and waiting to be called would only make me that much more late.

"You can't help me?" I asked.

"Sorry, you just have to get a number. Someone will call you shortly."

"Thanks."

I pulled a number and stood, waiting for it to be called. It didn't take long before my number was called. I walked to the window.

"How can I help you?" A plump Hispanic woman greeted me.

"I was supposed to have court this morning."

"What's your name?"

"Nicole Hayes."

"Looks like your court hearing was at 8 a.m."

"What? Are you sure?" I watched her scan her computer screen again.

"Yeah, it was this morning."

"I missed it." My heart immediately started beating ten times faster than it had been before I heard her words. "I was so sure it was 8:30," I said more to myself, but she could hear me. "So do I have a warrant out for my arrest or what's going to happen to me now?"

I wasn't even standing up straight anymore as I waited for her to respond. Both my elbows were on the low counter, and I wanted to cry. How could this happen? Why did I think it was 8:30 then? I couldn't go to jail. I had missed my own trial.

"It looks like the plaintiff didn't show either."

My mouth dropped in shock.

"Wait—Vivian didn't show?" I repeated.

Strange. Why hadn't she shown? It couldn't be due to a change of heart or not wanting to see me jailed and as far away as possible from Jayshawn. Why would she miss the opportunity?

"When neither you nor the plaintiff showed up, the judge dismissed the case."

Mendel, who had been standing behind me the whole time, asked, "And what time was the court supposed to be?"

The lady looked at him like didn't we just go over this, but said, "8 a.m."

"Wasn't that the same time we were giving tzedakah this morning?"

I glared at him, unsure. "The power of tzedakah."

Leaving the courthouse, extremely grateful for how things turned out, I immediately called Destiny   who of course had Jayshawn standing next to her when she answered the phone.

"Since you're calling, I gather they decided not to lock your ass up," she said, laughing.

I told her everything that happened and how I had missed the court hearing altogether—and so had Vivian.

"Do you think she got the time wrong too then, or what?"

"I really don't think so, because if that were the case, she would've arrived the same time as me or at least while I was still in the building."

"Yeah. You might be right. Unless she got the day wrong."

"Nah. She just didn't show up. I wonder why. Jayshawn, did you ask her not to come?"

I could see him doing that—but her actually listening, when she had caused so much trouble, was baffling.

"Your mom wants to know if you said anything to Vivian's ass to make her not show up today?" I heard Destiny say to Jayshawn.

"No," I heard Jayshawn say.

"Yeah, that's crazy, but hey—at least your ass don't gotta go to jail. Shit."

"Right. Because it was not looking too good."

Destiny made a few more jokes about prison and joked with Mendel about almost losing his wife to a prison wife.

"Okay. Ask Jayshawn if he's coming over."

"He said yeah, later."

The rest of the car ride was spent with me and Mendel discussing turning the spare bedroom into an actual bedroom for Jayshawn. Getting a dresser and a small desk for school—and other things to make it feel like a teen room. His room.

***

It was over.

The case was dismissed, and the one-year restraining order was over.

She had 780 Saturdays.

Impressionable years had passed.

What she left me with was 104 Saturdays before he turned 18.

I might have birthed him. Nursed him for the first six weeks of his life. But I was robbed of raising him.

He was my baby.

But he was her son.

I was making the bed, hanging up clothes in the closet, and about to start dinner for Her Son.

The End.
Well—
Does a story really ever end?

FINAL, AUTHOR RANT

If you're still here at the end of this book, thank you. And if you take anything from my story, let it be this:

Do not let the word **"open adoption"** fool you.

It sounds like it means continued contact, pictures, visits, updates. It sounds like a shared agreement between adults. It sounds like something flexible, kind, and modern.

But in **Arizona**—and in most of this country—open adoption is only as "open" as the adoptive parents want it to be. And unless the terms of that agreement are **filed in writing, approved by a judge**, and made part of the court's final order, **there is no legal obligation to keep it open.**

Let me say that again: if it's not part of a PACA (**Post-Adoption Contact Agreement**) filed with the court before the adoption is finalized, then legally, the promises made to you mean absolutely nothing.

I was Fifteen. I was vulnerable. I was told we had an open adoption. I believed it. I believed I would still see my son. That I could still be part of his life. That I wasn't giving him up completely—I was just giving him a "better" life. And when the adoptive family stopped answering? That was it.

No more updates. No more contact. No legal recourse.

And I want to be very, very clear—this happens to thousands of young women every year, especially Black and brown women, especially those who are in crisis, those who are poor, those who are told they're "doing the right thing" by choosing adoption.

We are praised for our strength and then discarded. The system wraps our trauma in a bow and calls it love.

What You Need to Know

- Consent is final. In Arizona, once you sign, your rights are gone. You can't change your mind unless you can prove fraud, duress, or coercion—and that is nearly impossible to prove in court.

- You will not get your child back if they break their promises. Courts rarely, if ever, enforce contact disputes.

- Open adoption is not legally binding without a court-approved PACA. Pictures, letters, calls, visits—none of it is guaranteed.

- Your child will receive a new birth certificate. One that erases your name completely.

- You are not "co-parenting" in an open adoption. The adoptive parents have 100% of the legal rights. You have none.

So Why Do I Still Speak Up?

Because maybe someone reading this is where I once was—young, scared, and being told that adoption is the best option. Maybe someone reading this is signing those papers today.

Please, slow down. Ask hard questions. Get everything in writing. Read the laws. Talk to someone who isn't benefitting from your decision.

And if you've already gone through it—if you're already living in the aftermath—I see you. You are not alone. You were not weak. You were manipulated by a system that profits off your pain. But your story isn't over.Ev

I wrote this book to take back mine.

**With love, rage, and hope for better,
Nicole Hayes**

MOTHER TO MOTHER

BEFORE YOU SIGN ANYTHING... ASK THESE QUESTIONS:

Is this adoption agency licensed in my state?

If not, walk away. Unlicensed agencies operate in legal gray areas.

Is there a lawyer representing only me? Not the adoptive parents or the agency?

You have the right to independent legal counsel. If they say it's "not necessary," that's a red flag.

Are the open adoption promises written into a legal PACA (Post-Adoption Contact Agreement)?

If not, you have zero rights to pictures, visits, updates, or contact after placement.

Can I change my mind after the baby is born? What's the legal deadline in my state?

In Arizona, consent becomes final shortly after signing. Changing your mind is nearly impossible unless you prove coercion or fraud.

What happens if the adoptive parents break their promises?

Most courts will not enforce contact. "Open adoption" is not co-parenting.

What support would I get if I keep my baby instead?

Any agency, couple, or organization offering to pay rent, buy groceries, or help during pregnancy should also help if you decide to parent. If not, they're just buying your baby.

Who is really benefitting from this adoption?

Ask it out loud. Look around the room. The answer matters.

EXTENDED WARNING SIGNS OF COERCION

If you hear or read these things—pause. You may be getting manipulated.

Emotional Manipulation (guilt/shame tactics)

- "You're giving your baby a better life."
- "Don't be selfish—think about the baby."
- "Real love means letting go."
- "You're not stable enough to be a parent."
- "A good mom puts her baby first."
- "You don't want your child to grow up in foster care, do you?"
- "Imagine your baby growing up with two parents and a backyard."
- "What if CPS takes the baby later? Better to choose now."
- "You'll feel proud of your decision one day."
- "You don't want to ruin the adoptive parents' hope—they're already so invested."

Financial Enticement (bribery disguised as 'support')

- "We can help with rent, groceries, maternity clothes…"
- "We'll take care of all your medical bills."
- "You won't have to worry about a thing during pregnancy."
- "Adoption is free—parenting is expensive."
- "We'll even help pay your phone bill!"
- Reality check: And then what? After birth, the "help" ends. And you've lost your child.

Ad Language to Watch For (from "crisis pregnancy centers" and agency posts)

These often appear on Facebook, TikTok, Google Ads, Instagram, even Craigslist:

- "Do you need a place to stay?"

- "Pregnant and scared? We can help."

- "Unplanned pregnancy? Free support and housing available."

- "Afraid you can't raise your baby? Let us help you choose a loving family."

- "Adoption is a gift. Be a hero to a waiting couple."

- "We'll walk you through every step of the process."

→ Translation: We will handhold you through surrendering your child.

Spiritual or Moral Guilt Tripping

- "This is God's plan."

- "Your baby was meant for someone else."

- "This is your chance to do something beautiful."

- "Adoption is a selfless act of love."

- "Don't kill your baby—place them in a loving home." (seen in anti-abortion centers that reroute into adoption)

Gaslighting Your Concerns

- "You'll regret trying to raise them when you're not ready."

- "Open adoptions are just like co-parenting." (false)

- "You can be like an auntie!" (also false)

- "You'll still be part of their life."

- "We'll never cut you off." (no legal backing unless in a PACA)

REMINDER:

Just because something is wrapped in kindness doesn't mean it isn't a trap.

If you're being offered housing, money, food, clothes, or love—only if you agree to adoption—that is not help. That is conditional assistance, and that is coercion.

REMEMBER:

- You have the right to say no.
- You have the right to change your mind—until you legally can't.
- You have the right to ask hard questions without being guilted.
- You have the right to be angry, confused, or scared.
- You have the right to parent your child.
- You are not selfish for wanting your baby.
- You are not weak for needing help.
- You are not broken for being in crisis.
- You are a mother. And your story still matters.